VGM's Guide to
Temporary
Employment

LEWIS BARATZ

VGM's Guide to Temporary Employment

A Practical Handbook for the Best Jobs

Library of Congress Cataloging-in-Publication Data

Baratz, Lewis.
　　VGM's guide to temporary employment : a practical handbook for the
best jobs / Lewis Baratz.
　　　　p.　　cm.
　　Includes bibliographical references and index.
　　ISBN 0-8442-4472-4
　　1. Temporary employment.　I. VGM Career Horizons (Firm)
II. Title.　III. Title: Guide to temporary employment.
HD5854.B37　1995
650.14—dc20
95-759
CIP

Published by VGM Career Horizons, a division of NTC Publishing Group
4255 West Touhy Avenue
Lincolnwood (Chicago), Illinois 60646-1975 U.S.A.

5 6 7 8 9 0 VP 9 8 7 6 5 4 3 2 1

Table of Contents

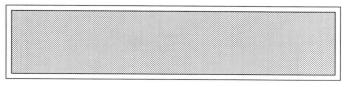

About the Author

LEWIS REECE BARATZ, PH.D., learned the ins and outs of the Temping game first-hand. His first Temp assignment was back in 1979, just after his freshman year of college. Finding himself a "paper pusher" at an insurance company in the days before automation, he swore he'd never go back to a corporate environment. Fifteen years later, Dr. Baratz has held hundreds of Temp jobs, with an experience portfolio that includes industries such as insurance, banking, health care, manufacturing, advertising, and mail-order. He's worked as a bookkeeper, database manager, ghost writer, secretary, administrative assistant, and guy-Friday.

Dr. Baratz was born in Brooklyn, New York, in 1961. By training, he's a music historian; by reputation, a chef; by conviction, a health and fitness junkie; and at heart, a writer. After teaching college and living in Brussels, Belgium, as a Fulbright Scholar and Belgian American Educational Foundation Fellow, he returned to New York after a thirteen-year hiatus to complete his dissertation. During that time, he conceived the idea to write this book, in order to share some of his experiences and insights. Never at a loss for words, the book is, as he puts it, "brutally honest." Its main purpose is "to answer all those questions the other books on Temping don't even ask, such as issues concerning personal finances, taxes, and just what the heck am I supposed to do in America if I need to see a doctor and don't have health benefits." The book also deals with hooking up temporary employment agencies, branching out on your own, and handling difficult bosses and co-workers.

Just at the time this book went to production, the author accepted a job as a statistical analyst at a financial services firm, which he thoroughly enjoys. "This is a company I can be proud to work at," he exclaims. He credits all his corporate savvy to his experiences as a Temp.

A *maiven* of the temporary employment industry and a scholar of Renaissance and baroque music, Dr. Baratz earned his BA and BFA degrees at the State University of New York at Buffalo, his M.Mus. at Southern Methodist University, and his Ph.D. at Case Western Reserve University. He also writes on health and fitness issues.

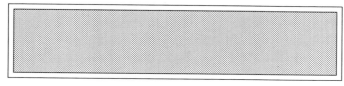

Acknowledgments

As with virtually every author at the time of completing his or her first book, there comes a moment of quiet reflection in which one can consider the many contributions of others. In this spirit, I should like first and foremost to thank my editor, Sarah Kennedy, for her encouragement and support. Bruce Steinberg, Media Relations Manager of the National Association of Temporary and Staffing Services, Inc., kindly furnished me with a myriad of materials and made several suggestions concerning terminology. Marcy Feltman of the City Commission on Human Rights in New York City supplied references for issues of discrimination. Linda Mayer created the chart on page 9 at her studio in Brooklyn, New York, and Selma Baratz spent many hours laboriously proofreading the different manuscript versions. "Sacker" and "the Comtessa" gave very special assistance. Finally, many thanks to those scores of temporary employees who shared with me their experiences and thoughts.

L.R.B.

Dear Temp...

Hi $$$—Immed. tmp pos avail w/midtwn brkg co. WP skls, dBase & spdsht exp (123), sten/FLH. Col A+. Fax res attn. Mr. Schlock 555-5555 EOE/M/F/D/V.

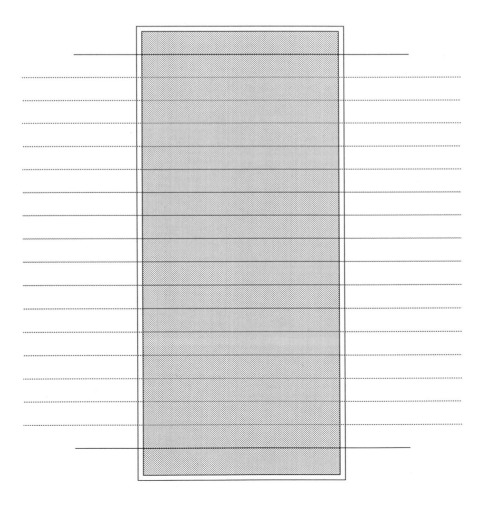

*S*o now what? You're new in town or home from college for the summer. Maybe you've just been laid off from your job or have suffered a personal tragedy. You need work. And fast. Nothing permanent yet, just something to tide you over. Perhaps you're retired but still want to put in a few days at the office or a full-time mom who's ready for a part-time job.

You open the Sunday newspaper and turn to the "Help Wanted" section. Voilà. You encounter what appears to be a coded message from the former KGB. Ads like the one above appear in newspapers across the nation every day. Businesses and temporary help companies advertising the chance of a lifetime, in a shorthand that often is ambiguous and confusing. But before you sit down to finalize your résumé, put a tank of gas in your car, or buy a ten pack of mass transit tokens, there are a few things you need to know.

First, what are they **really** advertising? Just what is "Hi $$$"? What kind of "WP skls" are required? What do they mean by "Col A+"? And just who is this Mr. Schlock? Does he need workers to fill specific positions or does he represent a temporary help company? What are your reasons for Temping? Will you find Temping to your liking? Will it accommodate your lifestyle? Should you work for a temporary help company or try to wing it by going directly to employers? What if you're seeking work for only a week or two? Can you balance your work schedule with your personal agenda? And can you make a career out of Temping?

In today's often uncertain economy, the temporary help industry has become one of the fastest growing employment sectors in the nation. With companies "downsizing," "rightsizing," and other "-sizing," full-time staff positions have become hard to find. With a greater number of applicants per position than at any time in recent memory, more and more people are considering temporary employment as a viable option—perhaps the **only** option—for the time being. The fact is, over a million Americans Temp each and every day. It's easy, relatively painless, and can be rewarding.

Temping is more than "table-waiting of the '90s." It is for many a career or lifestyle choice unto itself. For others, it is a means of survival until something more steady or fulfilling comes along. Temping also is a way of breaking into the work force, acquiring new skills, supplementing income, building a network, or just keeping busy.

To those new to Temping, securing personally and financially fulfilling temporary positions may appear to be a lost art form. But whether you're searching for a job in a large metropolitan area such as Boston or New York City, or a rural setting like Wilson, Oklahoma, there are plenty of commonalities. This book will guide you through the pitfalls and pratfalls of securing and living with temporary employment.

Written from an urban perspective, the tips and experiences shared herein are applicable to Anytown, U.S.A. This book shows you what it means to be a temporary worker, or "Temp," from the Industry's underlying vantage points: Client, Temporary Help Company (THC), and Temp. To help you become astute and successful we will explore the upsides, downsides, and flipsides of Temping. You'll see how to hook up with a temporary help company, how to acclimate to those first few assignments, and get to know the "Do's" and "Don't's" of temporary employment. And unlike other "how-to" books on the subject, this book serves as a reference tool for anyone who wants to learn more about Temping. The sources cited in the appendices can be found on hand or ordered at most libraries, throughout the country.

Whether you've come to Temping as a new worker, a returning worker, or an out-of-work worker, you'll see how to make the most of the Temping game. Temping has helped pay my bills all through college and graduate school, and continues to be my link with the corporate world. I've written this book to share some of my fourteen years' experience as a Temp clerk, word processing secretary, administrative assistant, and ghost writer. Temping is a respectable way to earn a living, and the many personalities I've met has certainly kept things exciting.

Note that while a temporary assignment will probably entail a "full-time," nine-to-five day, I use the expression "full-time employee" to signify a regular, "permanent" employee, because in this day and age, **No One Is Permanent!** Indeed, **"No One's a Permanent Employee" (NOPE)** will be a leitmotif of your working career.

Finally, you will have noticed by now I always begin the words "Temp" and "Temping" with capital letters. Why do I do this? To stress the importance of us Temps, that's why! As you read the pages that follow, you'll see how consequential Temps are to the American work force. We are gaining respectability at home and abroad, and the outlook for the future is bright indeed.

We are capital people and deserve to stand out in print and in real life!

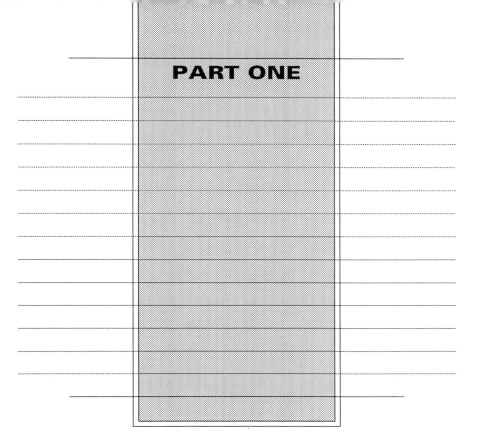

Background
Can I Temp?

CHAPTER ONE

What Is Temping?

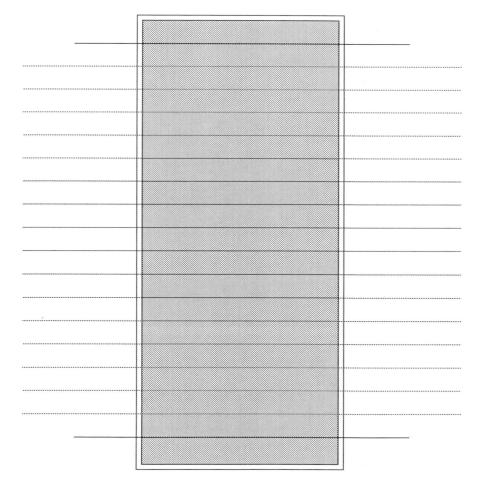

T emping is the act—or art—of providing labor services for a business, corporation, or other employer (the "client") for a finite or indefinite period. A temporary employee, or "Temp," is the individual whose services are contracted for the time period in question. Companies and businesses most often rely on Temps to substitute for full-time employees, for a variety of reasons, typically, vacation, jury duty, maternity disability, and sick-leave.

Temps are frequently hired as interim employees when a company seeks to fill a vacancy, as searches for support and executive personnel can take upwards of a month or more. Businesses also hire Temps to install new computer systems and to assist with special projects. Nowadays, companies occasionally downgrade full-time employees to the unenviable station of "Permanent Temporary Staff." This kind of restructuring relieves the company of its benefits obligations, including contributing to these employees' health insurance and retirement plans. Corporations of all sizes find Temps afford the most reliable and cost-effective solution to gaps in workflow.

Client Companies

Client companies usually requisition Temps through a third party Temporary Help Company (THC). Known colloquially as a "Temp agency," a THC is in actuality a "service," because unlike a "talent agency" it is neither on retainer nor takes from the employee a percentage of his or her gross pay.[1] The THC **is** the Temp's employer, and as such it does not represent the Temp the way a literary or theatrical agent does; rather, the Temp represents the THC every time he or she goes on a job assignment. THCs select the members of their Temp pools by carefully assessing the professional and interpersonal skills of applicants. The person who does the interviewing and sends the Temp out on a job is called a "work coordinator," "placement counselor," or just plain "counselor."

In the conventional third-party scenario, the client company approaches the THC to send them a Temp whose qualifications fit their job description. The THC then matches a Temp to the client's requisition and notifies the Temp of the work-related terms of the contract. The THC bills the client a negotiated hourly fee, apportions a fixed overhead and commission deduction, and pays the Temp the difference, which is agreed upon before the assignment commences. This translates to approximately one-half to two-thirds of the gross charge to the client, from which the Temp's federal, state, local, and social security (FICA) taxes, and workers' compensation insurance are deducted.

Some companies hire Temps without going through a THC. For highly skilled professionals needed to undertake technical projects or to implement new systems and procedures, client companies often turn to independent and subcontracted consultants. Consultants are experts in a given field and have the credentials to back them up. For more general office work, a large company may direct its human resources department to set up an internal, or "in-house," temporary help division so it can hire directly and train Temps who will work for them exclusively. Hiring Temps in-house saves them THC fees. The downside for the company is the extra paperwork and expense for maintaining tax and personnel records (further discussed in Chapter 8). But for the Temp, working in-house might draw a higher hourly rate and longer or additional assignments in familiar territory. There are also better opportunities for landing a full-time position at the client company, if so desired.

Temp Facts

A recent article in *Time* magazine revealed that nearly 34 million Americans—nearly **one-third** of the nation's work force—are **contingent workers** of one sort or another.[2] This umbrella heading comprises THC and in-house Temps, part-time workers, consultants, self-employed persons, freelancers, and all other nontraditional workers.

During Fall 1993, a staggering minimum of 6.3 million Americans held down part-time or Temp jobs on any given day. That's 200,000 more than in 1992 and a whopping 1.6 million over 1989.[3] All told, approximately 21 million people in America worked in some sort of part-time capacity in 1993, of whom 4.4 million sought full-time jobs.[4] According to the International Labour Organization, headquartered in Geneva, Switzerland, approximately 60 million people—one in seven of the world's work force—are employed in a contingency capacity.[5] Fourth quarter totals for 1993 suggest that short-term Temp assignments were held by 9 million to 11 million people in the U.S. alone, 80% of whom were women.[6] Of these, approximately 1.6 million worked through temporary help companies.[7] The annual receipts in 1992 amounted to an astonishing $24,900,000,000—nearly 22% higher than the previous year, with $16.5 billion in payroll receipts alone, and the numbers continue to rise. In terms of personnel, 1992 saw a 12.5% growth in temporary workers over 1991, while in 1993 the numbers swelled by another 16%.[8]

Consultants

The most highly experienced, hand-picked Temps are classified as *consultants*. Consultants are frequently contracted to set up or evaluate systems and operations especially in the computer, engineering, financial services, human resources, and health care fields. They often work with sensitive data the company does not wish to entrust to a full-time employee. Some consultants work independently as freelancers, but the majority are subcontracted through a consulting firm, which operates in the same manner as a THC, albeit with stricter guidelines. Consulting firms sometimes invite specialists in everything from aeronautics to zoology to join their payroll. Oftentimes they send a client three or four candidates for each position so they can choose the best fit.

Freelancers

Freelancers are independent consultants. They negotiate their work schedules and fees directly with client companies. A distinction in perception between a freelancer and a subcontracted consultant is that the latter often designs, enacts, demonstrates, or teaches a product or skill, whereas a freelancer does something for the company in lieu of a full-time employee. Freelancers need not be as highly skilled. They often are found at word processing stations or in marketing and training departments writing promotional copy or procedures manuals. Freelancers enjoy the freedom to pick and choose their employers and hours. What they don't like is having to sometimes battle corporate bureaucracies to get paid on time and the endless paperwork involved in filing their income taxes.

Leased Employees

Leased employees are the men and women who once thought loyalty and hard work would buy them a lifetime of security from a paternal employer. Not any more. They have been dispensed with, their health insurance and pensions "transferred" to an independent leasing company, then invited back as nontraditional workers while their security hangs in economic and socio-political limbo. Companies may lease out their employees in difficult economic times because poor market conditions

6

do not permit them to increase their prices significantly; they turn to payroll reductions to contrive an overall profit. Leased employees are not Temps, at least in theory; rather, they are supernumeraries whose compensation is the obligation of the leasing company. In reality, they, like Temps, can be terminated without notice and do not receive a "package deal" from the client company. It is up to the leasing firm to attempt to reassign them.

Floaters

The unsure, spartan '90s is also the decade of the *floater*. Floaters are both full-time and contingency employees that have no permanent desk. Descended from the "Gal" and "Guy Fridays" of the 1960s, these men and women are made to "float" from one station to another, as needed by the company. Full-time employees arrive at this situation when their departments have been phased out but they were not let go. They generally receive the same benefits as before, unless they have been leased, in which case their benefits packages have been renegotiated.

Other Temp Positions

Among THC Temps there are different kinds of job classifications. The largest among these are *general office support*. Falling into this category are:

- "Blue Collar" support such as mailroom clerks, messengers, and custodial workers
- Reception
- Clerical
- Telemarketing
- Data Entry
- Word Processing
- Secretarial
- Administrative Assistant
- Accounts Receivable
- Bookkeeping/Accounting/Other Financial

Manufacturing and Skilled and Unskilled Labor positions include:

- Assembly
- Construction
- Gardening/Landscaping
- Hospitality/Food Services
- Machinist
- Maintenance/Housekeeping
- Packaging/Shipping/Receiving
- Quality Control

Technical and Specialty/Professional classifications comprise:

- Actuarial
- Architecture/Drafting
- Banking
- Computer Programming/Software Engineering/MIS and LAN administration
- Computer Graphics
- Design
- Executive (Financial, Operations, Human Resources)
- Marketing
- Writing/Editing
- Illustrating
- Insurance
- Legal and Paralegal
- Dental Assistant/Hygienist
- Dentist
- Phlebotomy
- Nursing
- Medical
- Pharmaceutical
- Chemistry/Biology/Pathology/Other Scientific
- Research and Development

Permanent and Career Temps

Finally, there are the "Permanent Temps" and "Career Temps." These are people who do not desire full-time positions. They often enjoy personal agendas that do not lend themselves to a regular commitment to an employer. This group includes students, women with small children, seniors, and people pursuing creative endeavors such as writing, music, acting, and dancing.

Permanent Temps work directly for clients as in-housers. As such, the client is responsible for tax withholdings. There is often an understanding that the Temp will probably not progress to full-time employment. They are ineligible for the company's health insurance and retirement plans and are not paid for time off for vacation, illness, and holidays. Like *Career Temps,* they are not seeking full-time employments owing to personal agendas.

The following chart illustrates the two main venues for securing Temp assignments. If we think of Temping as a board game, the object is to move your piece from Temp to Temp Assignment. You, the Temp, shown at the top left hand corner, seek to arrive at the Temp Assignment. If you take the conventional route, along the way you will land

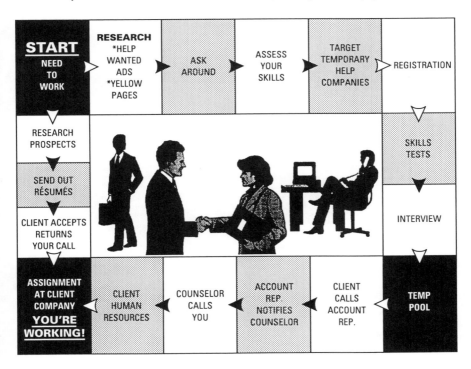

on the Registration, Skills Tests, Interview, and Temp Pool spaces before coming to Client Human Resources, which is the springboard for your ultimate move, the Temp Assignment. As with any game, however, there is a shortcut: a correct role of the dice can bring you directly to the Client Company as an in-house Temp or freelancer. Regardless of the path you choose, both lead to the Client Company, from where the need for your services originates.

CHAPTER TWO

Who Temps?

The reasons for Temping are as diverse as the people who Temp. For me, Temping was, until this past year, exclusively a summer event.

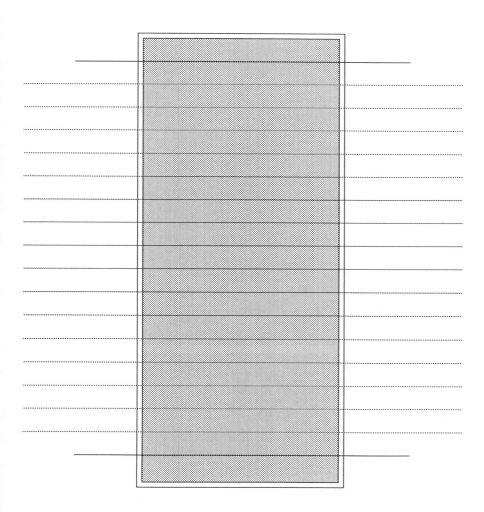

W henever I came home from college or had a break between writing jobs, I contacted my THCs to let them know I was available for work. I later Temped after completing graduate school because I couldn't find a job in my field. Temping afforded not only the possibility of buying groceries, but was also an excellent means for exploring industries and work environments I otherwise would not have considered. Consider some of the following circumstances and personal stories that bring people to Temping.

A Variety of Temps

College Students

College students qualify as seasonal workers because they must make the bulk of their money during the summer months. Temping brings in earnings to help pay for tuition and the Friday night pizza run. Students often have exceptional accounting, financial, and writing skills. Those who cannot or do not want to secure summer internships often can rely on their word processing experience to land high-paying Temp jobs. It is not uncommon for a student with any of the above skills to earn $5,000 or $6,000 in a summer. Taxes are calculated on projected annual gross income, but if total earnings are below $6,000 there should be a refund coming in April.

Recent Graduates and Teachers

A college degree is no longer an assurance of a decent job, as any recent graduate can tell you. Some young people go on to graduate and professional school right after completing their four years of study to either train for a specific career or to postpone facing a stagnant market. A sizeable percentage Temp while searching for full-time positions. For them, Temping brings a two-fold advantage because they can explore different work environments while earning money. Like college students, teachers often Temp during the summer to pick up extra cash.

Women

Some mothers with young children may find Temping the perfect chance to get out of the house, earn some money, and still have plenty of time to spend with their children. Many pick up skills on Temp jobs that can land them full-time employment once the kids are ready for day care or old enough to be on their own.

Wanda, 40, and a single mother of two, began Temping two years ago after being laid off from her secretarial job at an engineering company. She has experience with word processing, dictaphone, and stenography.

Although Wanda has worked steadily since 1992, she has had mostly short-term assignments. She is actively seeking full-time employment because she desperately needs a steady income and health insurance for her family.

Wanda often feels the THCs do not place her in long-term assignments because she is a triple minority, i.e., a woman of color and a single mom. But she is sensitive to current market conditions and gives her THCs the benefit of the doubt. She also is satisfied with her hourly rate and the actual number of days per month she works.

Dorothy, 58, the mother of three adult children, relies solely on Temping for her income. She has a secretarial background but had not worked in twenty-seven years.

Dorothy began Temping three years ago, just two days after her husband received notice that he was to be "laid off" from his construction job. Dorothy knew that "laid off," like "downsized," was '90s-Speak for fired. She has worked mainly long-term secretarial and light-typing assignments. Currently searching for a full-time position, she is concerned about financial matters owing to an impending increase in her health insurance premium.

Retirees

Nostalgia brings some retirees back to the work-place; the same holds true for boredom. Unfortunately, however, financial concerns bring back the majority. Our seniors have watched their promised pensions and health care benefits evaporate into smoke, and many have had to return to work just to make ends meet.

New and Returning Workers

People first entering or re-entering the work force often begin or complement their job search by Temping. Apart from the recent graduates, moms, and retirees, we find in the Temp pool people whose financial situations have changed, especially through divorce or the disability or death of a spouse. Women are hit particularly hard by these situations and, sadly, society often leaves them ill-prepared to take financial responsibility for their lives. Luckily, THCs are experienced in working with women who suddenly find themselves alone or responsible for supporting their families.

> Barbara's husband was killed in an auto accident in 1991. His life insurance benefits kept her going for a short time, but money began to run out.
>
> She had no prior work experience before she began Temping. She registered with several THCs and found work initially as a receptionist. Her excellent rapport with counselors and client managers opened the door for typing and data entry training. Barbara loves the diversity contingency work offers, but she has acceded to her eldest daughter's insistence she work for her, starting next year. Barbara says it was only by Temping that she was able to gain the requisite skills to manage her daughter's busy dental practice.

Ex-Military Personnel

The role of the American military is being redefined in the volatile and cost-cutting world of the 1990s. As in the private and service sectors, technology is attenuating the number of men and women needed in our armed forces. Many people leave the military with excellent skills, and Temping offers the opportunity to earn a decent living while retraining or exploring new industries.[9]

Professionals Seeking a Change

Lawyers, health care providers, pharmacists, bankers, and other professionals Temp or consult when they find full-time positions no longer to their liking. Some are officially retirees, others are still new to their fields and are shopping around for an advantageous situation. Some have family and personal commitments that preclude accepting full-time jobs. A small percentage have been displaced from the regular work force and must work on a contingency basis until they once again can secure full-time employment.

Writers, Performing Artists, and Other Artists

Almost every person involved in the creative and performing arts has experienced some sort of "survival," "day," or "civilian" job at one point or another. Young actors appearing in "showcases," hoping to have a director or agent spot them, often leave the studio after 5:00 P.M., grab a quick dinner, then head over to their "survival job" at the law firm until the wee hours of the morning, as do musicians between gigs.

The proverbial struggling actor/waiter is slowly being replaced by the actor-who-Temps. A good shift at a busy restaurant can bring in wages equal to or greater than those earned by a Temp, but waitering dictates working at someone else's schedule. A one-hour casting call can ruin an entire day, but Temping gives the opportunity to negotiate work schedules on a regular basis.

Why do so many people in the arts Temp? First of all, not every actor is going to land a regular "over-five" (i.e., a lucrative "speaking" role) on the daytime drama *One Life to Live,* so there are frequent gaps in employment. Furthermore, dance, theatrical, music, and vocal training take an enormous amount of time, energy, and money. Many people have to increase their earning power in order to pay for all the classes and supplies. Writers in-between books and assignments also need to earn additional money, but simply cannot commit to a year-round structured work schedule. Temping means sufficient income with the time flexibility demanded by auditions, photo-shoots, classes, meetings, research, and the like.

Some creative and performing artists are seasonal workers, others are permanent and career Temps. THCs on both coasts are well-aware of the magnitude of creative and performing artists in their Temp pools, and many try to accommodate them. Counselors enjoy working with creative people, as they tend to be well-educated, extremely personable, remarkably adaptable to new situations, and often can put to shame many full-time employees by their expert administrative skills and vast knowledge of software applications. For those who prefer not to sit behind a desk, THCs endeavor to send them out on assignments in the service and hospitality industries where they can put to use some of their creative energy.[10]

Charles, 35, has been a semi-professional opera singer for twenty-two years, commuting frequently between New York and Boston for teaching and concerts.

He has Temped doing clerical and bookkeeping work for twelve years to supplement his earnings. He prefers short-term assignments because of a busy recital schedule. Charles hopes to land a full-time teaching job at a conservatory as he is concerned about future stability. Having been "out-priced" by his private insurance carrier, he now subscribes to a health maintenance organization (HMO).

Joyce, 23, is an anthropologist turned actress. She lives with two roommates who are also struggling performers.

Joyce started Temping while still an undergraduate. Ten days a month she donned "civvies" and worked Temp receptionist and secretarial jobs to supplement her theatre and television earnings, but recently gave it up when she entered graduate school full-time. Joyce has only positive things to say about her THC, which she used exclusively. She got work whenever she needed it and has no complaints regarding any of the situations she encountered at client companies.

Change of Circumstance

Many people Temp because of a change of financial or logistical circumstances. Corporate downsizing has flooded the Temp pool with many talented and experienced managers. Male professionals are especially hard-hit by this, and here again, society has left them ill-prepared to pick up and start over as contingency workers. People new in town Temp to get a feel for their environs and to explore different possibilities. Finally, a growing segment of our population is living on the edge. THCs try to help these people, but it is still up to local communities to lend a hand with job training or, at the very least, help with procuring appropriate interview attire.

Carl, 46, is married and the father of two teenaged children. He owned and operated a small graphics and Local Area Network (LAN) installation company in

Texas comprised of himself, two full-time employees, and his wife, who worked part-time as receptionist and bookkeeper. The recession eventually closed his doors in April 1992. He thought he would have to leave Texas and come East but was able to hook up with a THC with a large professional placement division.

Carl has enjoyed numerous assignments in management information systems (MIS) and LAN administration both through a THC and as an independent consultant. His gross earnings are on a par with his previous, self-determined salary but his wife has not been able to find a job to make up for her lost income. Carl has re-incorporated himself as a small business and registered as a consultant with his local Chamber of Commerce.

Recent surveys indicate Temps on the whole are better educated than the full-time work force at large. A study published in 1994 by the National Association of Temporary and Staffing Services (NATSS) reported that 73% of all Temps have educational experience beyond a high school diploma. Of these, 39% have attended college, business, or trade school, 26% hold college degrees, and 8% have attended graduate or professional school.

The Survey was conducted in the Fall and Winter of 1993 by written questionnaire answered by 2,189 Temps.[11] Among the respondents:

- 78% temped to earn additional income
- 63% enjoyed the flexible work schedules
- 67% temped to improve their skills
- 76% hoped to land a full-time job through Temping

These last numbers show slight variance from the 1989 NATSS survey, in which 80% Temped to earn additional income, 77% favored the flexible schedule, 70% used Temping as a means for expanding or honing their skills. Interestingly, only 67% of respondents in 1989 hoped to land a full-time job through Temping, and this serves as an indicator of the growing numbers of full-time job-seekers out there. But 38% still wish to remain in a temporary situation even if offered a full-time job; 39% prefer to Temp indefinitely, and 76% are pleased with their work environment.

While the 1989 Survey indicated that the "typical temporary" is female and under 34 years old, with men comprising only 20% of the pool, the percentage of men in 1993 grew to 28%. Age factors also have changed. Currently, only 48% of Temps are under age 34, as compared to 57% in 1989. In terms of skill sets, 84% of Temps now hold word processing and data entry skills, 45% can use automated financial and bookkeeping hardware, and 42% can access a computer database.

Demographics in 1994 indicated a racial distribution of 82% Caucasian, 11% African American and other black, 6% Hispanic, and 2% Asian. Marital status comprised 36% single with no children, 15% single with children, 17% married with no children, and 32% married with children.

Finally,

- 52% said they were principal wage earners (44% in 1989)
- 49% were married, and 83% of these indicated a spouse who was employed full-time (43% and 80%, respectively, in 1989)
- 38% were offered full-time jobs through Temping (54% in 1989)
- 11% were *bona fide* retirees (12% in 1989)

Conclusion

In short, Temps are men and women, young, not-so-young, and seniors. Temps come in all shapes and sizes, and in every ethnic, racial, religious, and educational background. Some have high school equivalency diplomas, others have PhDs in medieval cosmology. Temps are actors, dancers, singers, musicians, writers, homemakers, and other persons pursuing alternative, creative, and personal agendas. Temps are people in the midst of career changes and individuals starting small businesses at home. Temps are flight attendants picking up extra cash during their monthly furloughs. Temps are among the "privileged poor"—those underemployed men and women who instantly can discern a Van Gogh from a Renoir, or communicate the differences between the timbres of the Chicago Symphony and the New York Philharmonic—and they are proud owners of million-dollar estates. Some are doctors, lawyers, accountants, and computer programmers. Others are scrambling to enter or re-enter the work force. Temps may bring years of experience with different software, dedicated hardware, office equipment, shorthand, dictaphone, legal secretarial work, and medical technology. One Temp might have mastered a complicated switchboard while another can balance a budget. Others may never have touched a typewriter but can edit reports. Some never worked before.

CHAPTER THREE

Is There Really a Need for Temps?

"Dupont plans to cut 4,000 jobs in U.S."
(*Wall Street Journal*, 14 September 1993, sec. A, p. 2[E])

"American Air will lay off 5,000 workers."
(*Wall Street Journal*, 15 September 1993, sec. A., p. 3[E])

"FDIC to close 15 offices, dismiss 3,300 employees."
(*Wall Street Journal*, 16 September 1993, sec. A, p. 14[E])

"More layoffs hurt morale, curb economy."
(*USA Today*, 20 September 1993, sec. B, p. 1.)

"Over half of Europe's big firms are planning work force cuts."
(*Wall Street Journal*, 21 September 1993, sec. A., p. 19[E])

The Current Work Force

Had enough? Notice that the above headlines represent **only one week.** And that's well over a year ago. We can turn to any week, any month in the past four or five years and see similar disasters announced. Alexander's, Gimbel's, General Motors, IBM, Kodak, US Steel, US West, American, Braniff, and Eastern Airlines, and Sears, Roebuck. The other computer giant, Apple Computers, announced plans to cut its work force by 16%, a total of 2,500 jobs.[12] Philip Morris intends to let go 14,000 people over three years,[13] RJR Nabisco will eliminate 6,000 positions[14]—nearly 10% of its employees—, and Xerox plans to terminate 10,000.[15]

Two of America's favorite bargain stores, Woolworth's and Kmart, plan to downsize by 13,000 and 5,350, respectively,[16] and American Cyanamid, Pfizer, Upjohn will slash its payroll by 7,000.[17] December 13, 1993 saw the harrowing revelation that Nynex is "considering" cutting 22,000 jobs.[18] 1994 began with the announcement that Bristol-Myers Squibb plans to sack about 5,000 workers,[19] while Pacific Telsis may shrink its Pacific Bell branch by as many as 10,000.[20] January 1994 also saw the sobering disclosure of GTE's plans to raise an $1.8 billion in pre-tax revenue while at the same time pink-slip 17,000 men and women, a full 13% of its work force.[21] Between 1989 and 1993 Western Europe lost 434,000 jobs in the textile industry alone,[22] and if that's not bad enough, Scott Paper is cutting its work force by 25%, 8,300 jobs because, apparently, there's a global overstock of toilet tissue![23] First quarter estimates for 1994 puts the number of Americans laid off on any given day at 3,106.[24] College graduates flipping burgers, pension plans drying up, and health insurance and long-term care benefits dispensed with by the stroke of a pen.[25] People who once believed they were secure at the work place are **out** of the work place, some for good.

Now it gets interesting. On the one hand, companies have had to streamline payrolls. On the other hand, industry has lost thousands of qualified managers, technicians, machinists, nurses, administrators, and so forth. The contributions of many of them are still needed, although the persons themselves have been dismissed. What does government and private industry do? Re-engineer and consolidate departments, cross-train, and hire some of their discharged employees back on a consulting, part-time, leased, or temporary basis.

Consulting firms and nationally-franchised THCs frequently supply the most talented people to companies in need of such services. Many THCs also cater to the manufacturing and retail sectors, as well as the hospitality industry. Because of the growing demand for a vast assortment of skills and backgrounds, today's Temps and placement counselors must be shrewd, practical, creative, confident, and highly adaptable.

Regardless, if the job you're filling is corporate, manufacturing, hospitality, medical, "paper pushing," or answering telephones, you cannot afford to alienate yourself—someone else can fill your shoes with only a phone call's notice. So always remember the three keys to getting work and making your assignments palatable, perhaps even enjoyable and rewarding: adaptability, congeniality, and professionalism.

Adaptability, Congeniality, and Professionalism

Adaptability is most important for your mental health. This is because you can find yourself at five different locations within a single work week. This means five completely different environments, managers, group of co-workers, and procedures, with precious little time to acclimate.

Congeniality means you can get along with almost anyone. Handling difficult people falls into place through your tact and diplomatic mien. A pleasant, but thick-skinned Temp will be called back frequently.

Professionalism means you show what you can do. Even if it's stuffing envelopes, you take your job and yourself seriously and work efficiently and honestly.

To answer our initial question, "Who Temps?," we need only to remember that the person who designed the company's mainframe computer system might have been a Temp, as was the woman who arbitrated Uncle Jerry's suit against his noisy neighbors. The boss who turned down your girlfriend for the cashier's job at the department store last Christmas might have been a Temp, as was the young doctor who removed Aunt Miriam's stitches after her appendectomy. One reputed author conceded that in just about any work environment, "the typists are Temps, the janitors are contracted, the engineers are consultants, and the manufacturing is farmed out."[26] Let's face it, even our government is made up of Temps: a President's assignment lasts for four years (usually), a Senator's for six (or any multiple thereof), and a Congressman for only two (at least in theory!).

Is Temping for You?

To answer this question, you need to evaluate your situation. Do you need work immediately?, Is your schedule flexible?, and Are you amenable to change? To find Temping rewarding you must bend with the wind, put your ego on hold, and make lemonade from any lemons encountered.

If you require a stable and structured work environment, Temping might not be for you. If you are a control freak, Temping is **definitely** not for you. The rules of the game change constantly. An assignment can end the same day it began or it can last for several months. The successful Temp is part chameleon, mind-reader, diplomat, and at times, therapist.

If you want work for a defined period of time, a week or two, the summer months, or longer, Temping is the best way to go. If you are a recent graduate or anyone else in the full throes of a job search, Temping can provide the much-needed income to get by as well as an opportunity to explore different industries and environments. Writers and performing artists, seasonal workers, and all other nontraditional workers often Temp for extra income.

Lawyers and corporate executives who have been "outplaced" from their regular jobs might attain temporary positions as interim officers, special projects coordinators, and consultants. Some leave their jobs voluntarily because the 9-to-5 scene has grown tiresome. And with earnings of up to $500 a day and up, they are more than well-compensated for their efforts.[27] Like anything else, patience and practice make perfect. Some assignments are more rewarding than others. Experiences span the gamut from the horrendous to the heavenly, and the awful to the awesome.

My first Temp assignment was at a large insurance conglomerate, in the days before personal computers, spreadsheets, and corporate restructuring. The work area resembled a Roman galley, a plain, open space with six aisles of twelve desks each. Fluorescent lights droned all day long, and getting up every few hours to buy a cup of coffee was the only diversion. The department was run by an inaccessible executive, and the two floorwalkers sauntering down the aisles all day contributed to the image of thralldom.

The task was to encode on various forms selected data from approved life insurance policies that would later be input by the adjoining department. The work was monotonous, but the assignment was to last the entire summer. Possessing neither insurance nor mainframe experience, I was constantly beckoning to a floorwalker for assistance. After the third week, the otherwise invisible vice president called a meeting with the floorwalkers and the three Temps. Owing to my complete lack of training, I was informed by her that my error ratio was 28%, and that I would have to improve or be replaced. Only 18 years old at the time, I was devastated. I had never been fired from a job—the fact that I never before held a full-time job didn't seem to matter. I managed to make it through the summer, even with constant admonitions from the data entry people that my handwriting was driving them crazy.

I did not understand that a discharge from a Temp assignment was different from being fired from a full-time job. There are no exit interviews, no termination of benefits, no period of anxiety seeking another position, no stigma or inconvenience other than to alert the placement counselors you're ready to start another assignment. While it is imperative to give it your best shot, it's not the end of the world if you leave or are dismissed from a situation that does not suit your skills or temperament. But there always has to be some give and take.

CHAPTER FOUR

The Upside, Downside, and Flipside of Temping

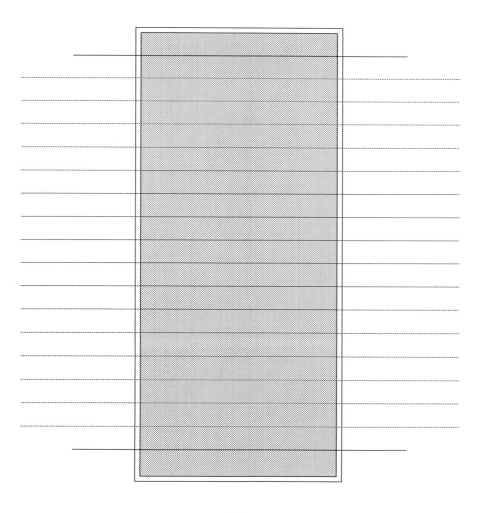

Don't waste your time asking if Temping is good or bad. If your financial and logistical circumstances demand it, then **do it.** And do it with a smile. Think of it in this most idealistic of terms: you will be one of the million and a half super individuals who on any given day are helping to rebuild America's economy and at the same time earn a respectable paycheck.

Many Temps believe they are completely unempowered. They perceive themselves as entirely at the mercy of the THC or the client company. Many feel they must go where the THC sends them or lose employment for that day or week. They see no opportunities to negotiate salary or direct concerns to the client company. True as this may be in many circumstances, there is a positive side. You often are more in control than you know. A good rapport with your THC can go a long way, and congeniality and know-how can empower you even in some of the most harrowing experiences. And we endure the good, the bad, and the neutral because it brings in a paycheck and gives us something to do other than watch yet another rerun of *Gilligan's Island.*

Upside

The paycheck is the bottom-line "Upside" of Temping. But let's not be so cynical. Temping has several other advantages including:

No Long-term Commitment

You are committed to the client company only for the duration of the assignment. It is advisable to remain at an assignment for the contracted period, but you can leave if you feel you are being taken advantage of, hassled, or frazzled. If the client appreciates your efforts they might invite you to extend your stay or request you the next time they need a Temp. They might even offer you a full-time position.

Flexible Work Schedule

Sometimes you just need a few days to yourself. The special needs of actors, musicians, and dancers have already been addressed. Orders for one- or two-day spots usually come in the morning of the job, so notify your counselor the afternoon before and make sure you're dressed and ready to go should the call come in for a 9:00 A.M. assignment.

If you are working freelance, you may be able to set your own hours or even work at home. Editors, proofreaders, technical writers, and graphic designers frequently "telecommunicate" with, or "telecommute to," their clients via modems and fax machines. A woman I know moonlighted for several years as a medical transcriptionist. A courier brought the day's documents and tapes over to her apartment precisely at 5:30 every afternoon. She faxed the finished product over to the physicians' group at 7:00 A.M. and gave the hard copies to the courier when he came by in the evening. Of course, most THC-dependent Temps do not enjoy this kind of arrangement, but gaining experience and increasing your network might bring you to a similar circumstance shortly down your career path.

Note, however, that the words "flexible" and "flexibility" are overused by authors writing about Temping, especially with regard to creative and performing artists. It must be emphasized that a commitment to an assignment is a commitment that must be honored, or, at the very least, renegotiated, at the discretion of the counselor. You cannot in all good conscience fail to show up for an assignment. Of course, there is no legal accountability, but don't expect to be sent out again.

Little or No Office Politics

Be suspicious of any company or department that claims it's just one big happy family. Families today more often than not are dysfunctional to one degree or another. There are frequent political and personality conflicts at play, some more stealthy than others. The only thing you can do is **stay out** of any perceived politicking. Don't share anecdotes about office personnel, don't tell one manager what you're doing for another, and don't be "cute" and try to endear yourself to a person or group of persons at the expense of (an)other(s). And don't talk about people in elevators, restrooms, or the cafeteria! As a disinterested party you must be cordial and respectful to everyone.

Non-Exempt Status

Executives, managers, and production crews often are required to work beyond the normal seven- or eight-hour workday. Lunch hours might be cropped down to a quick run to the company cafeteria for a sandwich gulped down on the way back to their desk via the nearest coffee machine. Special projects such as cleaning out file cabinets, supply room inventories, and preparations for audits, frequently involve weekend work as well.

Employees who do not receive additional pay for working overtime are called "Exempt." Support staff, hourly employees, union members, and most technical people are "Non-Exempt." It goes without saying that Temps are "Non-Exempt."

Temps generally are not paid for lunch hours, and your counselor will be up front about lunch-hour deductions. Temps should **never** be required to work through lunch without compensation. Ask the client supervisor on your first day how much time you should take for lunch; usually it's an hour. If anything other than an hour is indicated, notify your counselor and show the interval on your timesheet. Failure to deduct a lunch break is not only bad form, you may be required to reimburse the client and perhaps face dismissal or even legal action.

You will need to **clock** forty hours of work time before overtime kicks in. This means spending at least forty-five hours a week at work in order to qualify for overtime because of the lunch hour deductions, unless a special arrangement has been negotiated.

If you are asked to work beyond an eight-hour day or to come in on a weekend, make sure these additional hours are approved by your counselor and are reflected in your timesheet. Weekend rates are not necessarily at time-and-a-half unless they result in an excess of forty hours for the week or if an arrangement has been made between THC, client, and yourself.

> Ask your counselor about evening and weekend premiums. You'll probably earn a higher hourly wage.

If in doubt about hours, ask your counselor before accepting an assignment or when you make that first check-in call. In short, the more you work, the more you earn, and no one should expect you to "put in some overtime to get the project done" without prior notice and due compensation.

Potential to Learn New Skills and Procedures

I, along with the 67% reported in the 1994 NATSS survey, have often thought of Temping as on-the-job training. I've learned new software applications, virtually every kind of memory typewriter, photocopy, fax, and binding machine in existence, and have worked with numerous filing systems, expense account management, and have learned to access travel schedules and book reservations.

Each and every new skill increases your marketability. For instance, if you are proficient only at WordPerfect™ 6.0 but you're trained to use Lotus 1-2-3™ while on an assignment, alert your counselor to your new skill so you can be sent out on additional assignments.

Networking

The more people who notice your skills, the greater your opportunities for return assignments, freelance work, and full-time employment. Consider printing up your own business cards so you can present yourself as a "Word Processing Consultant," "Office Assistant Consultant," and so forth. Send a brief thank-you note to managers or other persons you worked with after completing a particularly good assignment. Managers have short memories when it comes to people no longer working for them, so keep your contacts current.

Downside

The integral downside of Temping is the lack of job security and benefits. There's also quite a bit of moving around and interpersonal challenges. However, this might not be such a bad thing. Consider some of the typical criticisms of working Temp:

Lack of Job Stability

Most of us like to know where we're going to be working on any given day. More importantly, we have a real need to be able to project our weekly, monthly, or yearly income so we can budget accordingly. Lack of job stability has several manifestations, but the bottom line is remuneration.

First and foremost is downtime. Temp assignments sometimes end abruptly on a Friday afternoon, making it difficult to line up work for the following Monday. And suppose nothing comes in on Tuesday? One unanticipated down-day is an inconvenience, but two or three days without work can mean a substantial deficit in gross income for the week.

It's all-too-easy to get angry and blame your THC for your having "lost" x-number of days' pay. The fact is you haven't lost anything, rather, you've gained nothing. Semantics, true enough, and the softening of the phraseology does little to pay the bills.

In all fairness, THCs try to avoid these situations, but there is nothing they can do when an inconsiderate client is involved. Temps must expect down-time as a consequence of this behavior. But registering with several THCs, keeping your contacts up-to-date, projecting a positive attitude, and continually sharpening your skills will increase your chances for work.

The worst aspect of the job security deficit is its imprecise annual net income projection and the subsequent hesitation to commit to large purchases, insurance, and residence upgrades. Regardless of your monthly income, your household expenses will more-or-less be consistent. And as an out-of-work Temp you do not necessarily qualify for unemployment compensation. "Entitlements" such as food stamps, Aid to Dependent Families, Medicaid, and Public Assistance are another story altogether.

Another consideration is that some companies are more pleasant to work for than others, and some locations are more preferable or accessible. Changing locales also can be an inconvenience. If you live in a "car town," only (no mass transit) commuting time, highway tolls, and the cost of gasoline will certainly come into play.

Few Benefits

Only in the United States and South Africa, from among all industrialized nations, are medical insurance and emergency leave considered "perks," privileges provided by employers for their full-time employees. For this reason, when most people hear the word "benefit" they think instantly of health insurance. Yet with the advent of public awareness and the government's recent recognition that our social ills have serious consequences on our economic fabric, the future promises to see a reorganization of the health care reimbursement system. The "benefit" of famiiy leave without pay was one of the first pieces of legislation President Clinton signed into law, and similar bills will surely follow in the next few years. But Congressional debates have shown us that a national health care policy will not happen overnight. Temps must thus take control of their situations. Of course, if you have health insurance through your former employer, university, parents, spouse, or, in some cities, domestic partner, you're in luck. You're also fortuitous if your THC offers a plan. If not, you are left with the decision of whether or not to subscribe to a plan on your own. Some programs are beyond the financial means of most Temps but there are still a few possibilities (see Chapters 7 and 9).

Assuming you can afford to get sick (or, to put it better, afford to get well), lost wages are still irreplaceable. Some Temps self-insure by putting away a small portion of their paycheck in a dedicated bank account just in case illness prevents them from working for a week or two ($30 a week for 48 weeks equals $1,440, about a month's take-home pay for the average word processor). Further, unlike our European counterparts, Temps usually don't enjoy paid vacation time, unless your THC offers a special incentive.

Office Camaraderie

Most people in the office will be pleasant; those who are not wouldn't be even if you were a full-time employee. If you must interact with them, just remember you are getting paid for a specific project and you leave the nonsense behind when the day is done.

The divergence in people one can work with reflects your particular job assignment and the client company, division, or office itself. Chances are you will not become buddy-buddy with a senior manager. Nonetheless, a pleasant work environment makes the day go faster, but keep in mind you are not there to make friends, just to get a job done and collect your due compensation.

Most Temps agree lunchtime can get tiresome if you constantly find yourself alone. Here are a few suggestions to break the monotony:

1. Visit the client company's cafeteria; you'll undoubtedly start to recognize a few faces after a week, and some of them might recognize you. Try to interact with people close to your age, sex, or job category.

2. Try to hook up with other Temps. One manager once called me the "Yeoman of the Guard" when she realized that for the past week a small confederation of Temps had been congregating near my desk everyday at precisely 12:00 noon. By the end of the week, our table in the cafeteria was more full than any other.

3. This phenomenon has my psychologist friends in disagreement although they all concede it works like a charm. Meet a friend who works in the neighborhood for lunch. When you return to the office, make a point of asking a full-time staffer where he or she went for lunch, then mention you just met your girlfriend Sally or buddy Bob, who's a secretary/banker/lawyer/vice president at Such-and-Such Corporation down the street. The reaction is usually one of awe. My gosh! You're human! You're not "just a Temp—you've got friends!" An invitation to join the regulars should follow shortly.

You may come across meetings and brainstorming sessions. These are perfect opportunities to feel left out. Many a Temp has watching a group of people trying to put together a budget report, proposal, memo, or a slogan, wishing they'd be given a chance to contribute some insight. If the full-time people don't want your input, don't offer suggestions, unless you are specifically being paid as a consultant. Other times, you might be invited to share your opinions or knowledge.

Feeling of Expendability

Finally, Temps are expendable. This hits office and industrial/manufacturing persons especially hard. In some corporate environments, one mistake, *faux pas,* or the wrong color tie, and POOF, you're gone! Other firms are so delighted to have someone who knows what he or she is doing, they'll keep you on for as long as you're willing to stay.

The decision to keep a Temp might be localized, which is good for you if your manager likes your work, or it can come down from the executive vice president's office, down to human resources, down to the divisional vice president, down to your manager. Stay on your toes, understand that an "indefinite" job can last for only a week or two, and stay in touch with your THCs to do your best to prevent any interruption in job assignments.

Flipside

Let's recap by juxtaposing the Upsides and Downsides of Temping. A lack of long-term commitment on your part is matched by no job stability. However, your employment status is not subject to the whims and misfortunes of a single boss, company, or industry, and you can bring your skill sets with you wherever you're assigned. The potential to learn new skills and procedures is offset by a feeling of expendability. For those hundreds of Temps who have felt left off the team, thousands more have networked. Flexible work schedules and the additional pay for overtime can be a consolation prize for the paucity of benefits.

Note that some of the larger THCs offer perks such as paid vacations, training classes, bonuses for completing a particularly long or grueling assignment, bonuses for referring applicants and clients, and discounted group health insurance plans. Ask around and read the company brochures. If you find yourself entitled to any of the above, discuss with your counselor. In short, there is no recipe for the life and experiences of a Temp. No two people are alike, no two assignments can compare. Be aware of this, be patient, and keep up the best attitude possible. Who knows, you might even love it!

CHAPTER FIVE

Keeping Up Self-Esteem

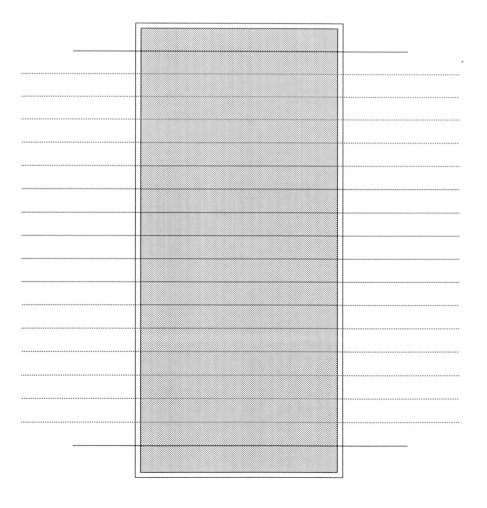

When the social historians of the future look back at America of the 1980s and 1990s, they undoubtedly will concentrate on the uncertainty and despondency so many of us today feel. Much of what we believed about the American Dream seems to have faded as we approach a somber dawn in our history. With one-fifth of our children living in poverty, young people now strive to live **as well as** their parents because **better than** seems unattainable.

America in the '90s

Witness the 51% divorce rate, the unfathomable numbers of adult children returning home, the numerous "power-tie, power-lunch, country-clubbed, pedigreed" males reduced to watching the soaps and accepting low-paying contingency work, while all they've worked for and trusted in seems to be evaporating around them, like suburban woods turned into failed shopping malls. The elderly see their benefits, promised and earned so many years ago, pulled out from under as they join the nearly 38 million under- or uninsured Americans.

Three groups have been hit particularly hard by the economic crisis of the past eight years or so. The 20-something crowd has found itself with degrees in one hand and a profusion of past-due bills in the other, sending out hundreds of résumés or wandering from job to job, often working second or third shifts and weekends as well.

The media calls them "Generation X" and their plight made the first page, column one, of the *Wall Street Journal* on July 28, 1993.[28] The reporter, Christina Duff, related that these young people suffer "from economic whiplash: They came of age in the ebullient, prosperous 1980s, yet were deposited—pricey degrees in hand—into the recession-squeezed job market of the 1990s." The article reported that almost a third of all persons graduating between 1990 and 2005 is expected to take a job that does not require a college degree. They do everything from serving cappuccino at the coffee houses they once frequented to dismantling church pews. Many moonlight and work weekends balancing a volley of part-time and temporary jobs.

The professional male gentry also has suffered. Over-educated, over-experienced managers out of work find they simply cannot secure jobs with pay comparable to what they once were earning. The *Wall Street Journal* also ran a story on their predicament.[29] Many men feel like failures and some experience depression and marital strain as a consequence of their financial situations and subsequent disruption of their households. A case in point that hit close to home concerns a friend of mine who recently received a promotion and a six-figure salary; he learned the following month that the purpose of his promotion was to put him in a supervisory position so he could phase out an entire division, while he himself was to be reclassified as a contingency worker before the end of the year. Senior citizens also have suffered from the cancellation of their pensions and long-term benefits.[30]

If you've chosen Temping as a career, the anxieties and fears experienced by many of us probably don't concern you much. But college students might be concerned with finding enough work to pay for the next semester. Persons recently laid off and women who have had to return to work can perceive entering the Temp market as an ordeal.

No one should take the attitude that they've been "reduced" to Temping. In fact, I am constantly amazed by the number of people I meet who are currently Temping or who have Temped. Everybody's story is different. Some love it, others tell me, "It kind of stinks, but hey, it's a living." Some say outright, "I'd rather be acting full-time," or in my case, "I'd leave this in a minute if a college teaching job opens." Others are hoping to launch into something "real," which I take to mean "full-time," and an equal number can't imagine doing anything other than Temping. The advent of the THC as standard fare in today's world means an outlet is there just waiting for you.

Get to it and go for it! If you have any doubts about that first step, then hop, jump, leap, or run. There's always something you can do, from surgery for some, to computer programming for others, to typing, grooming cats, collecting highway tolls, answering telephones, serving punch, or conducting surveys. Temping brings you to the workplace— any workplace—and half the battle is won. You will get used to being at the job site, expand your network, and get a chance to prove yourself.

There are literally millions of people eager and willing to meet the challenges and potential of working Temp. During the course of a year, the payrolls of THCs exceed those of the nation's largest employers, including AT&T, MCI, IBM, the Federal Government, and USAir. Figures have been cited for Manpower, Inc., one of the world's largest THCs. Articles appearing in *Time*,[31] *Fortune*,[32] *Working Woman*,[33] *The Progressive*,[34] and a host of newspapers including the *Chicago Tribune* and the *Los Angeles Times* attribute the number of persons involved with Manpower, Inc. to exceed half a million, roughly **twice the population of Luxembourg!** However, when considering that a THC counts everyone and anyone who worked for them for at least one day, the actual figure for 1993 averages to something between 80,000 to 112,000,[35] an eyebrow-raiser nonetheless.

Temp Success Stories

The folks profiled here have either found full-time employment through Temping or secured fortuitous arrangements with THCs and client companies.

Profiles

Paul, 26, a commodities trader. After graduating with a Master's degree in European Studies, Paul began Temping at a securities firm in Atlanta. His supervisor praised his writing and verbal ability and later transferred him to the International desk, with the consent of the THC. Paul was hired by the client company three months later and entered a one-year internship program. Dealing mostly with Scandinavia, his gross earnings have more than quadrupled.

Ryan, 29, an assistant marketing director, advertising. With degrees in music and literature, he began Temping four years ago as a clerk/typist. A long-term assignment a year later at an advertising firm turned into a full-time position as a copywriter. Although he took a small cut in gross earnings, he no longer had to shell out $2,250 a year on private health insurance. Ryan eventually was promoted to the marketing department, which he now manages.

Debbie, 32, a banker. After leaving a full-time job in securities, she returned home following a divorce. A THC sent Debbie to a bank office, where she processed bearer bonds. Shortly after, she was hired full-time and has been restored to her original title and salary level.

Chris, 28, a banker/programmer. Having received his BA in sociology, Chris decided against graduate school because he and his wife were expecting their first child. While searching for a full-time job, he Temped for seven weeks as a word-processing secretary, then for nine months as a Lotus™ programmer, a skill he picked up on his initial Temp assignments. Chris landed a job at an insurance company in the MIS department, and recently began to work at a major bank in the actuarial division. Although he earned a higher gross salary as a Temp, the vacation and health insurance factors were of prime importance.

Camilla, 38, an x-ray technologist. Camilla left her job as an assistant to a physician in private practice just after becoming pregnant. After a two-year hiatus, she attempted to return to work. Not able to secure a position with hours suitable for a single mother, she Temped as a bookkeeper for six months, after which she was sent on clerical assignments. She eventually hooked up with a medical THC (known in the industry as a *Locum tenens*), which placed her at a community hospital. Now she enjoys flexible hours and a higher gross salary than her colleagues.

Recapitulation

I hope this book so far has convinced you of a couple of things. First of all, **YOU ARE NOT ALONE!** There are thousands and thousands of good, honest, caring, people **just like you** out there who earn a living by Temping. Some are "Career Temps" pursuing alternative interests or creative endeavors. Temping to them serves only as a financial counterpart, a means of earning fairly steady money without a strong and long-term commitment to a given employer, apart from the THC. Others Temp for the myriad of reasons outlined before and then some.

We are men and women. We are ageless. Our experiences in life are priceless. We have high school diplomas and doctorates. We are innocent and we are shrewd in the ways of the world. We are in the prime of our health and we are living with physical challenges. We are people. And we are America.

> You are among friends! Rejoice then in knowing that the backbone of America owes many a vertebra to people like you.

Temping is an honest, ethical, and popular way to earn money. No one is giving you a handout. You are working hard, you are showing them what you can do. There is plenty to be proud of.

> Go for it! Psyche yourself! Talk with friends! Have faith in yourself. And be patient . . . There is work out there, and a little know-how does go a long way.

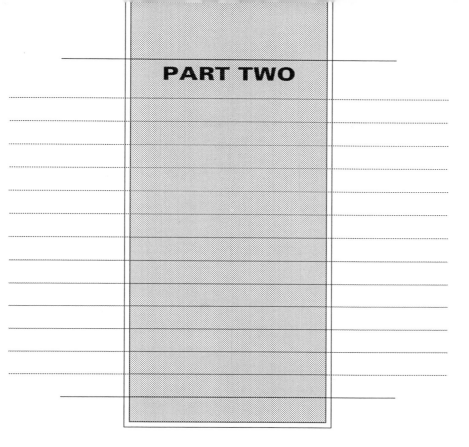

PART TWO

Money Matters
Really, It Does!

CHAPTER SIX

Making Ends Meet

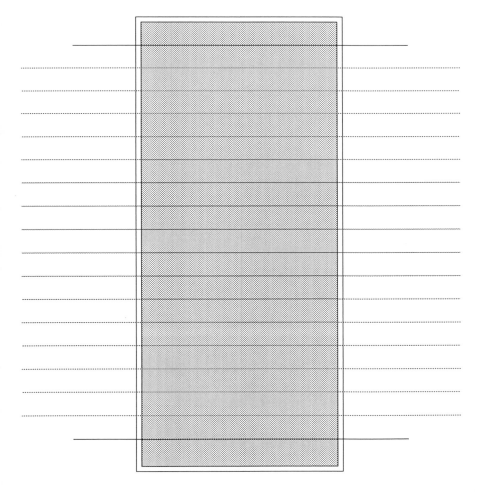

Temping usually won't lead you across the rainbow to the pot of gold but, assuming steady work, you should be able to at least meet your basic expenses and then some. Consultants, freelancers, and legal and medical Temps usually enjoy greater leeway in negotiating hourly wages. Persons working through THCs generally earn the same hourly rate for each job assignment within a given work classification.

THC payment structures are based upon job classification and the shift of the assignment. For instance, word processing rates are higher than data entry, and night and weekends shifts usually pay a premium rate. Temps with graphics and computer programming experience are well-compensated, and Temp software engineers often earn more than physicians working Temp. That's why you need to hone and expand your skills at every opportunity and make sure your counselor is kept up-to-date.

Budgeting

Everybody's budget is different, and before you start Temping you should have a clear idea of how much money you need to get by. The basics for determining your budget are rent, groceries, utilities, telephone, and the size of your household. **Always remember to allot approximately one-third of your gross income to the Tax Man in your budgeting!**

Let's say you just graduated from college and are searching for that first job. Maybe you'll move back to your hometown or try a new city and need to rent an apartment. Chances are you'll take the cheapest arrangement possible, maybe move in with a friend or find a roommate through a notice in the newspaper. You can always move someplace nicer once you land a better paying job. But supposing you were laid off from a $60,000-a-year job as a computer programmer and are now entering the precarious realm of the consultant. Of course, some consultants will earn very well, but others will work for what they once considered "chump change." Perhaps divorce or death has suddenly left you with a mortgage. You certainly will need more money than a recent college graduate (assuming his or her student loan repayment is not prohibitive).

There are other things to consider. Are you a Shop-a-holic? Do you talk on the phone non-stop to relatives in Melbourne, Australia? Is your health insurance premium making you ill? Do you wish your student loan processing center would repossess your college degree? Do your credit card bills dance the Tango in your dreams? Are there more urgent expenses such as medical bills or the care for a child or other loved ones?

Now supposing you're like 99.9% of us and have average rent, average grocery bills, average utility bills, and average credit card bills. You certainly can get by on a Temp's compensation if there are only brief intervals between assignments.

Because Temps can never be sure of their income, some weeks will be better than others. If you moonlight or do weekend work you can live the life of the rich and famous on payday. But there will also be weeks with plenty of down-time, and you've got to make sure you have enough money put away for the essentials.

Set out your primary needs (rent, groceries, utilities, telephone, essential toiletries, transportation, and pet supplies, if applicable), your secondary needs (health insurance, credit card bills, clothing, not-so-important toiletries), your tertiary needs (entertainment, "just-gotta-have" clothing, eating out, and that $40 cologne), and miscellaneous expenses. If you are on your own this scheme requires little alteration, but if other people are in your life, especially children and other dependents, the situation becomes more critical.

It's not so much a matter of earning money first and trying to budget than it is finding out what you need and then trying to earn it!

Consider a bare-bones budget for someone living with low rent. Actually, it's my budget from a couple of years ago when I lived in squalor with two other recent college grads in an apartment.

Lewis's Expenses—June 1992

Rent	$ 380.00
Electricity	48.06
Gas	13.00
Telephone	52.00
Groceries	180.00
Transportation	62.50
Credit card bills	65.00
Student loan payment	93.80
Subtotal:	$ 894.36

Toiletries	$	20.00
Household items		20.00
Laundry		12.00
Dry cleaning		14.00
Postage		6.00
Clothing		51.62
Subtotal:	$	123.62
Lunch/coffee	$	60.00
Newspapers/magazines		12.00
Books		23.50
Compact discs		31.65
Dinners out (2x)		40.00
Take-out food (3x)		20.00
Video rentals		9.00
Haircut		15.00
Miscellaneous		10.00
Subtotal:	$	221.15
TOTAL:	$	1,239.13

My targeted gross income for the month was $1,876, about $470 a week before taxes. I divided this number by 35, the ideal number of hours per week I needed to work, and came up with $13.43, which we can round off to $13.50 an hour. Factoring in a one-third tax deduction, the net is about $9 an hour. We can double-check the equation by multiplying $9 by 35 by 4, which brings us to a weekly take-home pay of $315 and a monthly total of $1,260. The budget has been met, with $21 left over for an emergency (or a couple of movies). But I still spent many sleepless nights wondering how I could purchase health insurance that didn't carry a deductible that would drive me into bankruptcy, or buy a car while I still had some hair left on my head. For me, however, the most important consideration was moving out on my own.

My budgeting formula differs somewhat from that included in an insightful discussion on setting freelance writing fees found in the *1994 Writer's Market*.[1] This takes into account a base figure comparable to a full-time employee's salary for a particular service, in this case writing, plus "fringe benefits, taxes, etc.," "overhead," and a "10% profit margin." The paradigm uses as its base figure an annual gross salary of $26,000, which is divided into 2,000 hours (40 hours a week multiplied by 50 weeks—a "vacation" of 2 weeks has been factored in). The result is $13 an hour, to which is added 33% for taxes and insurance, etc., overhead based on annual expenses of $5,000, and the "10% profit margin," which comes out to $4.29 + $2.50 + $1.30 for a total of ($13 + $8.09 =) $21.09 an hour.

The formula is useful, although I find the added-in amounts high. Try to come up with your own plan that takes into account your needs, a full-time employee's salary, and another $1.10 or so an hour to cover the cost of private health insurance (approximately $1,800 a year) for yourself, more if there are other family members involved.

Equal Pay for Equal Work?

Keeping my budget in mind, I saw no alternative other than to accept a long-term in-house position at a company I shall refer to as the ABC Sprocket Corporation, Inc. My gross hourly rate of $15.38 was contrived by the client company, which based my compensation on a full-time employee's salary of $28,000. Furthermore, everyone at the company was paid biweekly, which made the exact nitty-gritties just a bit more complicated.

A full-time employee shared the mysteries of her paycheck with me as our annual salaries were congruent in terms of hourly wages. But that's where the similarities ended. In juxtaposing the two, notice that "Lonnie S. Temp's" paycheck is somewhat more hefty than that of "Pat Q. Full-Time."

At first glance, it looks like "Lonnie" is living the good life, pulling in more money than a full-timer. Seventeen dollars a pay-period more, which amounts to $8.50 a week, $34 a month, $408 a year to be exact. Or perhaps not.

First of all, "Lonnie" is a Temp, so dismissal can come at any time. Pat's "deficit" of $8.50 has bought a full day's vacation, amounting a "gift" of $107.69 before taxes. Both have paid identical taxes, but "Pat's" deduction of $15 provides major medical, hospitalization, and a substantial medication benefit. Finally, "Pat's" *ADD LFINS* deduction of $1 per week provides over a hundred grand in insurance money in the event of accidental death. And "Pat's" boss doesn't think twice about the *de minimis* benefits such as using the fax or copying machines for personal business every once in a while. But if "Lonnie" were to approach the fax machine with personal documents a verbal hanging, drawing, and quartering might be the consequence thereof.

ABC SPROCKET CORPORATION, INC.

INTERNATIONAL DIVISION
555 LOUVAIN STREET, NEW BRUNSWICK, ID 11111
EMPLOYEE NAME: PAT Q. FULL-TIME
PAY PERIOD 05-01-93/05-14-93

PAYROLL ACCOUNT

5543450956809

EARNINGS	HOURS	AMOUNT	DEDUCTIONS		YEAR-TO-DATE	
REGULAR	63|00	969|24	FICA TAX	81|35	GROSS PAY	11900|08
VACATION	7|00	107|69	FED TAX	104|60	FICA	898|89
			STATE TAX	51|76	FED TAX	1557|37
			LOCAL-1 TAX	4|61	STATE TAX	573|87
			LTD	6|25	LOCAL-1	50|95
			MEDPLAN	15|00	MEDPLAN	165|00
			ADD LFINS	2|00	ADD LFINS	20|00
			ADD DISINS		ADD DISINS	
			COSTOCKOPT		COSTOCKOPT	
					OTHER	
TOTAL EARNINGS	70|00	1076|93	TOTAL DEDUCTIONS	265|57	NET PAY	811|36

ABC SPROCKET CORPORATION, INC.

INTERNATIONAL DIVISION
555 LOUVAIN STREET, NEW BRUNSWICK, ID 11111
EMPLOYEE NAME: LONNIE S. TEMP
PAY PERIOD 05-01-93/05-14-93

PAYROLL ACCOUNT

0051126326809

EARNINGS	HOURS	AMOUNT	DEDUCTIONS		YEAR-TO-DATE	
REGULAR	70|00	1076|93	FICA TAX	81|35	GROSS PAY	11900|08
VACATION			FED TAX	104|60	FICA	898|89
			STATE TAX	51|76	FED TAX	1557|37
			LOCAL-1 TAX	4|61	STATE TAX	573|87
			LTD	6|25	LOCAL-1	50|95
					MEDPLAN	
			MEDPLAN		ADD LFINS	
			ADD LFINS		ADD DISINS	
			ADD DISINS		COSTOCKOPT	
			COSTOCKOPT		OTHER	
TOTAL EARNINGS	70|00	1076|93	TOTAL DEDUCTIONS	248|57	NET PAY	828|36

CHAPTER SEVEN

Benefits

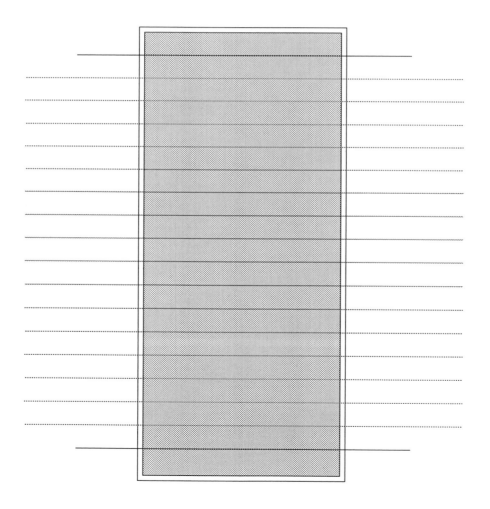

In the "Old Days," employers paid their workers by cash or check at the end of the week. Few deductions were made, apart from taxes (most of the time), and if the employee was paid in cash it was easy to neglect on the government's allotment. Our current social security system continues in most instances to place the onus of health insurance, family leave, vacation, and sick days on employers, and as such many small businesses cannot afford these discretionary benefits. There is virtually no Federal accountability, so the worker is out of luck. Benefits are privileges that differ from the Federally mandated "entitlement" programs set up for seniors and the disenfranchised. They are thus key components of compensation.

Compensation Packages

Today, three distinct factors are figured into full-time employees' compensation packages: salary, benefits, and job security. Chief among the benefits is health insurance. This is followed by vacation time and "sick days," dental insurance, and finally, life and supplemental disability insurance. "Hidden" or "invisible" compensation averages out to over a third of an employee's gross salary. One writer calculated a gross salary of $32,300 carries "hidden" benefits of $12,402, with unemployment and workers' compensation accounting for 8.8%, retirement and incentive savings for 5.5%, life insurance for 0.5%, health insurance for 9.9%, paid rest periods for 2.4%, paid time off for 10.5%, and miscellaneous for 0.8%.[2]

In addition to discretionary benefits, full-time employees of larger companies often enjoy various "perks," including *de minimis* benefits such as the use of the company cafeteria, free promotional material like company sweatshirts, umbrellas, clocks, and pens, and the use of telephones, fax, and photocopy machines, and so forth. Larger corporations might also offer stock options, profit-sharing, child care, use of cars, cash bonuses, incentive savings plans, retirement plans, on-site medical exams and vaccines, full payment of membership dues for professional societies, and tuition reimbursement.[3] But health insurance continues to be the crux of all this and the main concern of workers across the country. For example, in 1986 health benefits issues accounted for 18% of strikes nationwide but only three years later the number skyrocketed to 78%![4] Current estimates attribute over 90% of all work stoppages in America to this issue. So aren't you glad you're going to Temp and don't have to worry about these things? The lesson from this is that the few extra dollars a Temp might earn cancels out many times the written and understood benefits most full-time employees enjoy.

Of course, not everyone in the office understands this. I've had people pour out their ire at me upon discovery that my hourly wage was slightly higher than theirs. And no discussion about benefit factors could abrogate their anger. Some people forget, or never understand in the first place, the amount of money their employers spend on their benefits. So **never** discuss compensation with anyone at the work place, with the exception of a sympathetic boss who is in a position to give you a merit raise or bonus.

Unemployment Insurance

The specific criteria for collecting unemployment benefits and amount of compensation are determined by each state, in accordance with guidelines set by the Federal government. The national average is somewhere around 79% of your former gross salary for a total of twenty-six weeks. However, some studies have shown that **less than 50%** of qualified persons are actually receiving their benefit. And unlike Common Market and other European nations, the United States does not extend unemployment benefits to students, part-time workers, seasonal workers, farmers, and dependents of unemployed persons. Indeed, if while you are unemployed you register for academic or vocational courses in an effort to improve your skills, you will lose your eligibility. To make matters worse, unemployment compensation is considered **taxable income.** This may change, however, if proposed legislation clears Congress in 1995.[5]

You cannot collect unemployment compensation if you voluntarily leave your job. Fortunately, labor law recognizes that quitting because of hazardous conditions or harassment constitutes just cause. In short, you either have to be fired or quit because of intolerable conditions. However, being terminated because of illegal activities or a serious violation will disqualify you. You must actively be seeking work. In today's world, this means being registered and in daily contact with job placement services. (The same holds true, incidentally, for deferrals or forbearance on student loans.) Finally, you had to have earned the minimum "base rate," as set by your state. To determine this amount, contact your state labor department.

Of course, the sticky matter for Temps is what if you've earned, say, $12,000 for the first six months of a year and then the summer crunch hits and no assignments are available? Supposing that $12,000 was the result of tireless efforts on your part and five different THCs? Who is responsible for approving your unemployment insurance? Who determines that being registered and in touch twice a day with ten THCs demonstrates you really are seeking work? A bureaucrat might ask why you, a lawyer who once earned $75,000 a year, turned down a one-day Temp job as a receptionist for five bucks an hour.[6]

Therefore, you've got to do your own legwork. Go to your local library as soon as you think you might be entitled to unemployment compensation and get yourself informed. And when you go to the labor department, bring along photo identification, your social security card, and a few paycheck stubs.

CHAPTER EIGHT

Taxes

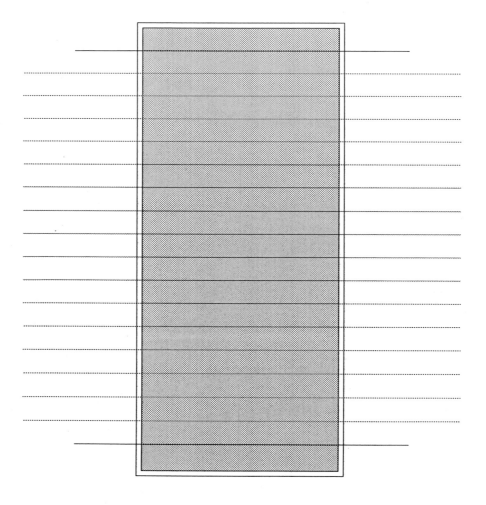

HCs and leasing companies are required by law to deduct income tax withholdings from the paychecks of Temps and issue W–2 forms based upon the allowance indicated on the W–4 form. If you have appraised yourself "Exempt" or have indicated an inordinately high number of dependents or allowances on your W–4, someone from the THC's accounting department might intervene to "assist" you in recalculating your situation. However, as long as the THC adheres exactly to what you have indicated on the W–4 and sends you your W–2 or other appropriate earnings documentation, they bear no liability for any problems that might arise between you and the IRS or your State Department of Taxation later on. To avoid any inconvenience, save your paycheck stubs.

Income Taxes

Filing income taxes should be no more painful for Temps than for anyone else. If you're single with no dependents, rent rather than own a house or apartment, work exclusively through THCs or clients on an in-house basis, and have few or no work-related expenses in excess of the standard deduction, you most likely can file Form 1040EZ. If you're married (legal or common-law), have a domestic partner who's also a wage-earner, have dependents, own property, and/or earn in excess of $50,000, Form 1040 or 1040A might be more appropriate, along with applicable Schedules. In any event, **read the relevant IRS literature** and, if necessary, confer with a professional income tax preparer. Be aware that this can be costly if you've earned money on consulting jobs. Despite my small earnings in 1992, having H&R Block do my filing cost me $97, but at least I had the peace of mind knowing that everything was filed accurately and legitimately. You can also consult current literature at your local library, such as the instruction manuals supplied by the IRS and the tax guides published annually by Consumer's Guide, H&R Block, and J.K. Lasser, among others.

IRS forms can be confusing, especially to first-time tax payers. But **under no circumstances** should you become too frustrated to pursue the matter and dodge your obligation. This will only lead to trouble. Follow two simple rules and life will be easier:

1. As stated earlier, always deduct one-third of your gross income in your mind towards your taxes.
2. If you have any questions, concerns, frustrations, or fears at all, contact a professional income tax preparer.

Types of Forms

The first tax document you will encounter is the W–4, "Employee's Withholding Allowance Certificate." Each time you register with a THC you will be required to fill out a copy. The W–4 is the basis upon which your withholdings are calculated. You must also update your W–4s at the beginning of every calendar year. Use the "Worksheet" attached to the W–4 to determine your exemptions and additional withholdings. I strongly recommend you do not indicate "EXEMPT" in the belief you can "settle up" with the government later on. This will only lead to grief down the road. If your earnings for the year are small, you most likely will receive a refund.

The W–2 is the form sent to you by your employer(s), assuming you've filed a W–4. As defined by the IRS, income includes wages, commissions, prizes, awards, honoraria, research grants, severance pay, tips, interest, and sick pay.

Most THC and in-house Temps, subcontracted consultants, and leased employees will find their tax situation fairly straightforward. Freelancers, however, will have a harder time of it and should strongly consider working with a professional income tax preparer unless, of course, you happen to be an accountant or bookkeeper yourself. For them, one of the many "1099" forms will come into play. The 1099s report income for which no W–4 has been filed. Many of us are familiar with the 1099s for dividends (1099–DIV) and interest on savings accounts, bonds, and Zero-Coupons (1099–INT). Retired persons might amass 1099–Rs if they receive pensions or maintain an Individual Retirement Account (IRA). If you've sold stocks or bonds, you'll receive a 1099–B. If you've collected unemployment compensation, you'll get a 1099–G, and social security benefits are indicated on a SSA–1099. Most freelancers, however, will receive from their various client companies a 1099–MISC, which is the standard income reporting statement for wages not appropriate for the W–2.

The essential difference between the W–2 and 1099–MISC is that no deductions have been made from earnings reported on the 1099–MISC. The amount indicated reflects your **gross income,** from which you are liable for federal, state, and local taxes, as well as social security withholdings (Federal Insurance Contribution Act, or "FICA"), which can be as high as 25% in certain circumstances. In addition, independent contractors and other self-employed persons are required to pre-pay their estimated income tax on a quarterly basis. To be safe, check with a professional tax preparer.

Note that the IRS is not particularly fond of employers reporting compensation on the 1099–MISC. You should have clearly established criteria as to the circumstances under which you will accept payment as a freelancer versus as an in-house Temp. The reasons are obvious:

1. You do not want to be hit with a devastatingly high tax bill come April 15th.

2. As a 1099 worker, you are completely responsible for the full share of your social security taxes.

3. The IRS feels that: (a) some companies try to avoid paying their regular contribution to your social security tax by shifting their in-house Temps to 1099 status, and (b) it is sometimes difficult for the IRS to determine accurately the gross income some 1099 workers have actually earned in a given year (the same holds true for waiters, doormen, and other persons who count on tips as part of their compensation).

Regarding item 3, the IRS and state taxation departments are closely watching the payrolls of companies that regularly hire in-house Temps and freelance consultants. The clamp-down came about because some companies hired back former employees on a contractual basis—although they reported their compensation, they issued 1099–MISCs instead of W–2s. The rule of thumb for employers to avoid an audit is to report on a W–2 any employee who works on premises and save the 1099s for freelancers and consultants who work at home or for brief periods.[7]

Always attach your W–2s, 1099s, and other earnings statements to your tax filing, regardless of forms filed (e.g., 1040, 1040A). In addition, Schedules might be needed if you have had high medical costs, property acquisitions, sales, appreciation or depreciation, and so forth. Consultants or freelancers working out of their homes should consider filing Form 8829, which may entitle them to deduct part of their rent or mortgage payments; Schedule C or C–EZ can be filed if you've earned $25,000 or less, experienced business expenses of not more than $2,000, and do not employ any persons other than yourself. Schedule C or C–EZ can also be used in conjunction with, or in lieu of, Form 4562 to deduct automobile depreciation and gasoline (currently 29¢ per mile) if you use your vehicle primarily for business.

This brief explanation of income tax concerns provides only an overview of the kinds of complexities, opportunities, and responsibilities involved. Discuss your case with a professional tax preparer if you receive anything other than a W–2, have accepted independent consulting or freelance work, or have questions about filings.

CHAPTER NINE

Health Insurance

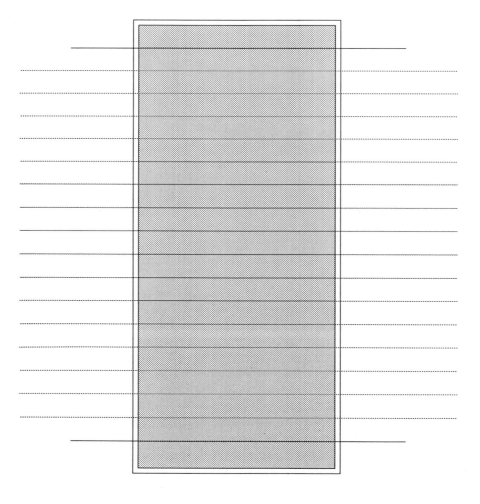

Despite all the recent discussion about health care reform, we still do not have guaranteed access to affordable primary medical care, specialty surgeries, psychiatric and substance abuse treatment, or prescription drugs. Some states, especially California, Florida, Hawaii, Minnesota, and New Jersey, are ahead of the rest of the country in their innovative insurance programs for lower- and middle-income people. Also New York and California have responded particularly well to the needs of uninsured persons with HIV infection. But there is neither universal nor optimum coverage offered by government agencies, so as a Temp, chances are you will have to fend for yourself.

Buying Your Own Insurance

If you opt to purchase your own health insurance, you can set yourself back about some $2,000 a year. You cannot get help from government agencies towards your purchase nor can you deduct the full amount of premium on your tax returns.

The jury is still out on this issue, and current premium allowances are not generous. Medical expenses are subject to a 7.5% floor of your gross income, as indicated on Schedule A. Schedule A does not specify insurance premiums, but their cost can be factored into the 7.5% floor. Prior to 1994, self-employed persons could deduct 25% of their health insurance premiums outright, with the remaining 75% of premium costs claimed as a medical expense on Schedule A. This all changed on January 1, 1994, when a congressional bill terminated deductions for self-employed workers. However, attempts are being made to restore the premium write-offs retroactively to 1994, and increase deductions to 50% in 1995, 75% in 1996, and 100% in 1997.

Here's how it works. Let's say you earned $22,000 last year but had to buy your own health insurance. You opted for a health maintenance organization (HMO) and live in a low-risk area, such as eastern Wyoming, so your premiums are low, figure about $90 a month, which comes to $1,080 a year. You had the flu and had to see the doctor twice, but because you saw an HMO-affiliated doctor you paid only $5 per visit. But medication wasn't covered, so you had to pay $45 for something to unclog your stuffy nose. Your total out-of-pocket expenses, including your premium, amounted to ($55 + $1,080 =) $1,135, which is $515 below the allotted 7.5% floor so you cannot claim medical deductions on Schedule A. If, however, you earned $14,000, had no medical insurance, came down with a particularly virulent case of flu, and had two wisdom teeth extracted later that year, you might be faced with this model:

Taxable Income	$14,000
Floor ($14,000 x 7.5%)	1,050
Medical Costs	1,275
= Doctor visits (2)	$ 175
= Chest X-ray	85
= Blood/Lab	45
= Medication	120
= Oral Surgery (2 teeth)	850
Medical Expenses	$ 1,275
7.5% of Gross	$ 1,050
Deduction	$ 225

You have a floor of $1,050, leaving $225 which can be deducted on Schedule A, assuming reinstatement of the 25% premium proviso.

It seems appalling that someone with earnings of $22,000 pays approximately $6,160 (28%) in Federal income tax, not to mention state and local taxes, and is supposed to take care of his or her own medical costs as well as those of any dependents. This practice also has proven itself economically disastrous. Furthermore, few private insurers reimburse for preventive medicine. This is incongruous with the most basic logic, because an ounce of prevention is truly worth a pound of cure.

The government supplements the elderly with Medicare, although this program does not pay for prescription drugs, the price of which often brings seniors to their knees. Medicaid helps the most disadvantaged segment of our society, but with the first few paychecks earned they lose their qualification for this "entitlement." As with virtually every other social service, you are faced with an all-or-nothing predicament.

One interesting question that has become fashionable to ask in the '90s is "How much insurance do I need?"[8] To be considered are: 1. Your current health and health history; 2. The current health and health history of your spouse and dependents, if any; 3. Your lifestyle (Do you smoke? Are you at risk for heart disease, diabetes, cancer, HIV, genetic illnesses, etc.?); and 4. The possibility of having children in the foreseeable future (as some carriers will not cover pregnancy-related expenses if conception has occurred prior to issuance of a certificate of insurance).

Some Safe Possibilities

Before plunging into despair, consider this. Can you still obtain health insurance through your former employer? If you did not have insurance through your former place of employment (or did not have a former place of employment), what about through your university, if you are a college student? Can you be added to the policy of your parent(s), spouse, or domestic partner? If you are over age 62 you might qualify for Medicare, or perhaps you are entitled to Medicaid because of the previous year's earnings.

Federal law mandates that if you are terminated from a full-time job you can still continue your health insurance plan for up to eighteen months, but at your own expense. This legislation is called the Consolidated Omnibus Budget Reconciliation Act of 1986 (COBRA). The advantage is that if you are already receiving or have recently received medical care for a particular illness you do not have to worry about termination of such care for a year and a half. The unsubsidized premium can exceed $300 a month for individuals, more for dependents. Some persons who are "downsized" are offered a compensation package that will include at least some of the premium paid by the former employer.

If you're a student, you probably can subscribe to your university plan, or if have a working parent, you might be able to obtain health insurance through his or her employer. Some insurance companies terminate the benefits of dependent children when they turn 21, while others offer a rider for children who are full-time students up to age 26. Still other companies offer adult children of insureds reduced premium or automatic approval as long as the parents continue to subscribe.

Enjoying one's spouse's benefits is an integral element of our social system. The policyholder's premium will increase, but not necessarily double. Assuming no chronic illness or recent "pre-existing condition," there should be no problem in adding a spouse to an insurance policy. Domestic partnership is considerably more tricky and eligibility, if any, varies from city to city. Common-law spouses and same-sex couples generally have to prove they have lived together for at least three years. But some large corporations have begun to realize that in order to attract and maintain a small but significant number of creative and dedicated employees, they must end discrimination and extend benefits to same-sex domestic partners.

Seniors can consider joining the American Association of Retired Persons (AARP), an organization that provides a wealth of information to persons over age 55. Many amateur and professional societies offer some sort of group health insurance plan. I was able to purchase an affordable short-term policy through my membership in a professional organization. Virtually any society with at least 20 members can approach a broker for assistance in securing a company to underwrite a group plan. Note, however, that premiums may vary by zip code.

The insurance industry justifies the premium structures by factoring in the cost of care as well as the overall risk component of different locales. Geographical factoring also can be used to discriminate against individuals who are presumed to be "high risk" for cardiovascular disease, certain cancers, and HIV infection because of where they live, regardless of their lifestyle and overall health. Some states are now requiring a "community rating" approach in which individual policies must be offered to all applicants at the same premium, regardless of the applicant's age and medical history.[9] As always, check with the carrier in question.

And If You're on Your Own . . .

If you don't want to take the risk of living without health insurance while Temping, there are still a few possibilities. The giant corporations such as Blue Cross Blue Shield offer the most comprehensive benefits, but the premiums can exceed $2,500 a year. This option is recommended for those who want the greatest choice in doctors and services and the highest reimbursement ceiling. Some THCs will offer a 50% premium reimbursement on certain plans if you work for them for a prescribed amount of hours within a set number of months and continue working for at least three full weeks after that. Although not ideal, this arrangement helps out considerably. Read the THC's literature upon registering and discuss the guidelines during your interview.

Managed Care

In terms of plans, we seem to be moving more in the direction of "managed care." This umbrella heading includes HMOs and paid providers organizations (PPOs), which involve lower premiums but more restrictions. HMOs generally require subscribers to utilize a particular medical facility for their primary care needs and permit them to use only member hospitals. However, subscribers may pay as little as $2 or $5 per doctor visit and only $5 or $10 for prescription drugs, depending upon the kinds of plans offered in your state. PPOs offer a wider choice in selecting primary care physicians, but you have to make a higher co-payment. Among the better-known HMOs are Kaiser Foundation Health Plan Inc., Prudential Health Care Plan Inc., CIGNA HealthCare Inc., United HealthCare Corp., U.S. Healthcare Inc., Aetna Health Plans, Health Insurance Plan of Greater New York (HIP), Humana Health Care Plans, Health Net, and PacifiCare Health Systems. PPOs include USA Health Network, The Affordable Medical Networks, Admar Corp., MultiPlan Inc., Preferred Health Network, CAPP Care Inc., and Aetna Health Plans. Check insurance guides at your library for addresses and telephone numbers to ascertain eligibility. You can also contact the National Insurance Consumer Hotline, which offers a free booklet on private insurance policies. Staff members are available to discuss specific issues 8:00 A.M. to 8:00 P.M. weekdays EST at (800) 942–4242.

Private Health Insurance

For private health insurance, I initially contacted ten carriers and asked them for the following information:

1. Type(s) and terms of medical and dental insurance offered;

2. Territories covered;

3. Exclusions, including pregnancy and pre-existing conditions; and

4. Other pertinent information.

The companies are located in Florida, Georgia, Illinois, Iowa, Ohio, Nebraska, and Pennsylvania, and service the entire country. **Only one** responded to my inquiries, which tells me they either are not interested in covering Temps or they are extremely protective about their lines of business.

The company that responded was Time Insurance Company. While it is inappropriate to recommend this company over others solely on the basis that it replied, the fact remains that a company spokesperson stressed that Time Insurance Company is the nation's largest under-writer of short-term individual medical policies. In addition, my personal experience as a policyholder has been completely satisfactory.

Time Insurance Company offers a short-term policy of up to six months in any given calendar year at a premium that is substantially lower than regular individual policies. The policy carries a critical care aggregate of $2,000,000 and goes into effect immediately upon receipt of premium. Should you file for and receive benefits for a specific illness, you will be eligible to continue treatment for that condition for a full calendar year after the policy has expired, at no additional premium. However, these policies are not designed to substitute for year-round coverage because the six-month on again/off again approach can be a recipe for disaster should any serious illness or disability occur.

Premium is determined by the type of plan chosen. As this book goes to press, one may choose from among deductibles of $250, $500, $1,000, or $2,500, and a co-payment rate of 20% or 50% over the next $5,000 in medical expenses. Once the ceiling for covered out-of-pocket expenses is met, Time Insurance Company pays 100% of medical costs incurred up to the $2,000,000 ceiling. As with all short-term policies, the premium takes into account the base rate and the sex, age, and zip code factor of the applicant. Zip codes factors (1995 rates) range from a multiplication of the base rate by 0.60 for several counties in Indiana and throughout Iowa, Nebraska, North Carolina, and North Dakota, to 1.80 for those areas of California with zip codes beginning with 900–907 and 918. Thus, a male aged 28 living in Utah opting for the 80/20 plan with a $500 deductible would pay only $33.60 a month (December 1993), but if he moved to the District of Columbia his premium would jump to $57.60 a month. Note that these plans are not available to residents of Alaska, Hawaii, Maine, New Jersey, and New York. For further information contact the company toll-free at 1–800–800–1212, ext. 8335.[10]

Group Plan

Even if your THC does not offer a health insurance plan, you may be eligible for a group plan if the THC is a member of the National Association of Temporary and Staffing Services. You may be able to subscribe to the NATSS-affiliated policy underwritten by Albert H. Wohlers & Co., located in Park Ridge, Illinois. In cooperation with underwriters such as Time Insurance Company and Fidelity Security Life Insurance Company, Albert H. Wohlers & Co. administers various plans. Their short-term plan is available to persons needing coverage for a period of 30 to 180 days.

The terms are straightforward. A $250 deductible applies, then the 80/20 co-payment kicks in for up to $5,000 in expenses incurred, after which the company pays 100% of medical expenses up to the cap of $1,000,000. One "re-application" is available during a calendar year. The plan is also available to spouses up to age 65 and to dependent children under 19. The long-term plans are available to "full-time staff employees . . . and for temporary employees who have been employed twenty hours a week for three months."[11] Eight options are offered, four each for the comprehensive and economy plans. Premiums are determined by sex, age, deductible, and geographic factoring. Because review of applications can take a month, the Company recommends first enrolling in a short-term plan for thirty days.

With both the short-term and the long-term policies, policyholders are billed directly. Those Temps who can receive a partial insurance benefit from their THC should discuss the details with their counselors. You can also call Albert H. Wohlers & Co. directly at 1–708–803–3100 or 1–800–323–2106. A company official reported that residents of Vermont, New Hampshire, and New Jersey may be excluded from the long-term plan due to state insurance regulations, but alternatives are being explored. In short, address all queries directly to the company.

Shop around and choose a plan that fulfills your needs and fits your budget.

CHAPTER TEN

Of Special Concern to Women

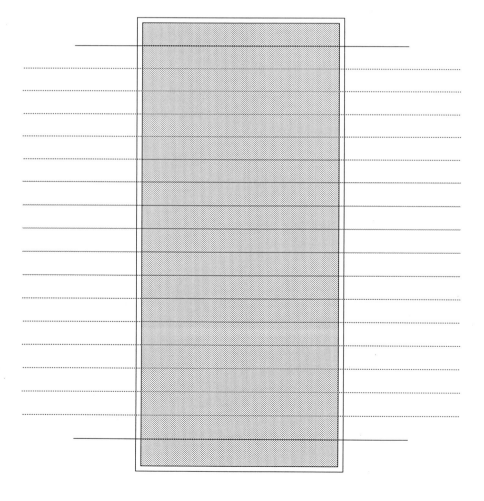

"**A**nother day, another fifty-nine cents" is more than dark humor. It's a sad reflection of the economic subservience to which women in our society have been consigned. Despite the growing number of women attorneys, bankers, neurosurgeons, and members of the board of directors, the earning power of women remains lower than that of men across all segments of society.

The Unequal Status of Women

A woman is more likely to live in poverty than a man and is less likely to have investments in her name. Divorce or death of a spouse generally has greater financial impact on women than men in corresponding situations.

Why? Certainly women are not less intelligent than men. Rather, they are victimized frequently by a society that carries vestiges—if not the outright prejudices—of a time when women were supposed to rely entirely on their husbands to support them. True, the wife often kept the household budget, but the portfolio and other investments were the husband's domain. It was amusing to see a woman ignorant of the contents of the family safety-deposit box or know the consequences her new diamond necklace had on the family savings. Writing the checks for rent, auto loans, insurance premiums, and college tuition was simply not lady-like.

Certainly, many of these attitudes have changed and the idealized world of Eisenhower-era America, as portrayed by Hollywood, simply has no bearing whatsoever in today's difficult and often violent world (it probably didn't have much relevance back then either). However, it is odd that even in the early grades girls are still expected not to perform in mathematics and the sciences as well as boys. (The irony is that teenaged boys are frequently ridiculed for taking home economics courses, which they often wish they did when they have to fend for themselves.)

The situation has gotten so out of hand that support groups are cropping up around the country to teach women how to take what is rightfully theirs.

In short, the days of equating financial dependence with cuteness are gone forever, even though society still resists the old traditions such as the dry cleaning establishments that charge women more than men— even when they bring in men's clothing to be cleaned—and the unisex hair salons that have separate price schedules for men and women, regardless of the length and amount of time spent on the hair in question.

Equality in Temping

Fortunately, most THCs are gender-blind. It is simply economically disastrous for them to attempt to place women in lower-paying jobs because of the negative repercussions. No woman, or for that matter, no man or woman, with computer experience is going to be placed as a receptionist unless there truly are no other jobs available. A woman will not be offered a rate lower than a man for the same job classification, as the THC is **not** going to risk a discrimination suit or jeopardize its profit potential.

Temping is thus a safe haven for women in terms of hourly wages. For both men and women to learn how to manage their finances better, there are public libraries, seminars, and night-school classes. Therefore, take control of your life. Don't be afraid to ask questions.

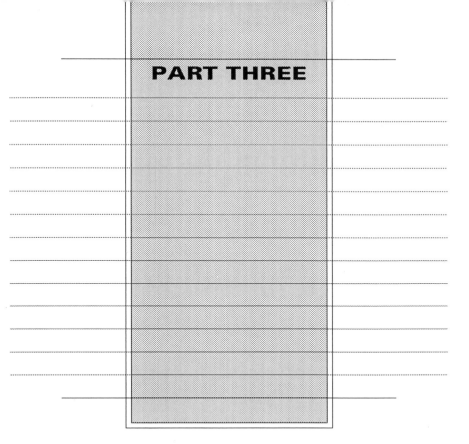

PART THREE

Getting Started
The THC Connection

CHAPTER ELEVEN

What Does The THC Do?

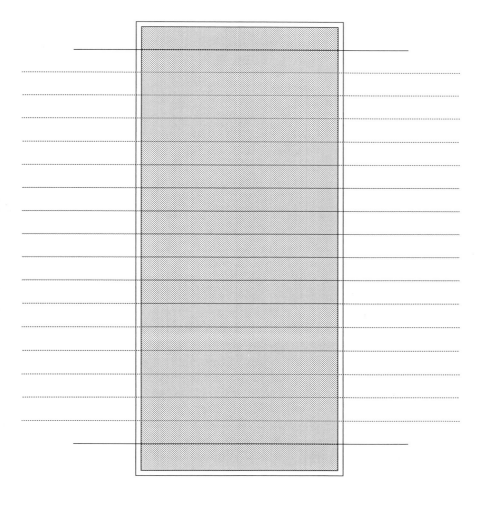

Put simply, the Temporary Help Company (THC) attempts to get you work for a day, week, month, or indefinite period. It supplies employers with temporary personnel they cannot add to their regular payrolls owing to considerations of budget and practicality.

The Role of THCs

Most of the nation's 17,000-odd temporary employment offices take responsibility for:[1]

- Recruiting, testing, and evaluating applicants.

- Establishing and maintaining relationships with client companies.

- Assuring quality control by checking up on the Temps they send out and offering compensation if the client is dissatisfied.

- Paying for workers' compensation and disability insurance for their Temps.

You become an employee of a THC with your very first assignment. Obviously, it is employment in a nontraditional sense. You are not beholden to the THC for any longer than an assignment lasts. You are not given a formal orientation process on the operation of the client companies, do not receive a benefits package, and are not paid for any time you do not work, unless your THC offers a bonus program.

It is up to you to let the THC know when you're available for work. Assuming you have demonstrated good skills, attitude, and appearance, they will try to accommodate your work needs and schedule. Once you have successfully completed the initial assignment, signing up for work is only a phone call away.

With some 17,000-odd THC offices to choose from, where do you begin? What do you do if there are well over a hundred in your vicinity? What if there are only two? What about going directly to client companies? If you don't have an infinite amount of time and energy at your disposal, the THC arrangement is the most convenient and surest route.

THCs are legitimate businesses. Some, however, are more aggressive than others in procuring work, setting compensation structures, following antidiscrimination legislation, and arbitrating work-related conflicts fairly and diplomatically. Only a very small number are inadequate; if you feel yours is unprofessional, terminate your dealings with them.

What Is NATSS?

The National Association of Temporary and Staffing Services (NATSS) is an organization made up of experts in the field of temporary employment. Located in Alexandria, Virginia, and with chapters in nearly every state, Puerto Rico, and the District of Columbia, NATSS compiles and shares industry data, keeps up with government legislation and IRS guidelines, advises new and long-established THCs on maintaining and upgrading their product, and negotiates on issues germane to the industry in an effort to make easier the lives of Temps and their employers. About 80% of the temporary help industry payroll is generated by NATSS members.

NATSS was founded in 1966 as the Institute of Temporary Services. Its mission then and now is to "ensure that members could provide flexible employment opportunities to the work force while simultaneously supply competent temporary help services to businesses and industry."[2] NATSS currently works with about 1,100 THCs operating approximately 8,300 offices nationwide, 85% of total industry sales. NATSS "provides its members legal, legislative, and industry-related educational information as well as exclusive member discounted services." In addition to statistical reports, monographs, and hosting annual conferences, NATSS puts out a quarterly journal called *Contemporary Times*. Begun twelve years ago as a forum for sharing industry data, *Contemporary Times* also contains a question and answer dialogue, chapter news, and advertisements. The journal **is not** written for Temps themselves, but serves as a resource for THC personnel who desire to keep up-to-date in this forever changing and growing industry.

NATSS is headed by 5 officers and 19 members of the Board of Directors, all of whom are owners or senior officers of THCs; 16 regular staff personnel oversee the day-to-day operations, update and circulate the extensive data network, and organize conferences and special events.

Selecting a THC

So, you've decided to take the THC route. Smart move, especially if you don't have the luxuries of time and inside contacts. Probably the best way to begin is with a referral. Do you know someone who's Temped? Do you know which THCs your former employer used? Ask around. If this proves to be a dead end, you will have to do your own leg work.

The Search

The obvious place to begin your search is in the "Help Wanted" section of your local newspaper. This is the means by which THCs recruit the lion's share of their Temps. The greatest number of listings are in the Sunday edition. Also check your local Yellow Pages under "Employment Agencies," "Employment Contractors—Temporary Help," and "Employment Services—Employee Leasing." The newspaper ads, however, are more current and will give you a better idea of the types of positions handled by the THCs. In addition, the number of separate ads placed by a THC is a good indicator of the volume of positions available. If you do not find your area of specialization listed, call some of the larger THCs and ask if they handle computer programmers, medical and legal personnel, and so forth, or could recommend one that does.

The number of THCs varies from city to city. Most cities with a population of at least 30,000 will boast two or more nationally established or franchised THCs such as Kelly Services, Olsten Temporary Services, and Manpower Temporary Services, in addition to a handful of smaller, localized THCs. Large and small THCs have their advantages and disadvantages, so I recommend registering with at least one national and one or two locals in the beginning.

Some friends and acquaintances tell me they prefer working with the national companies because they've gotten steady work and slightly better pay rates. Franchised THCs can be particularly convenient if you move to a new city—your test scores and work history can be transferred to different branch offices. Others prefer the independent THCs because these services, as "locals," often enjoy special relationships such as exclusive-use connections with the city's or district's businesses, especially manufacturers and regional banks, and are promoted by their Chamber of Commerce.

The number of THCs situated in a particular locale gives you an immediate idea of demand and competition. The 1993 *Manhattan Yellow Pages* lists 149 THCs comprising 130 listings for general office support, 2 for nursing, 3 for accounting, 3 specifically geared towards Apple/MacIntosh® systems and graphics, 5 food service contractors, 2 messenger services, 1 for direct mailing service, 2 for medical services, and 1 for executive placement service. Surprisingly, **Atlanta, Georgia** outnumbers New York with 175 THC listings. The Atlanta breakdown (1994) is:

General Office Support	117
Accounting	10

Advertising/Media/Public Relations	2
Aerospace/Energy/Petrochemical/Telecomm	1
Claims	2
Construction	8
Medical/Nuclear Imaging	5
Hotel/Food/Hospitality	1
Human Resources/Recruitment	1
Insurance	1
Legal (Lawyers/Paralegal/Secretarial)	5
MacIntosh®	2
Mainframe/PC/LAN/MIS	8
Manufacturing/Design/Engineering	11
Security	1

The significance of Atlanta's temporary employment industry is that the city was among the first to have the industry included in the "Real Connection Consumer Tip" hot-line. Sponsored in this instance by Southern Bell; you can call into the hot-line by dialing 404/633–3336 from a touch-tone phone. When prompted, enter either 1335, 1336, 1337, or 1338. Each extension activates a tape that gives a sixty-second "infomercial" on different aspects of Temping. The recording concludes with inviting you to press "#" (the pound sign) to be connected with the sponsor.

Extension 1335 gives a brief run-down on the function of the THC (which it refers to as "the agency"), how it screens employees, job possibilities, and opportunities for training. The extension is sponsored by Expertise Temporary Personnel, Inc. Extension 1336, sponsored by Dunhill Temporary Systems of Atlanta, Inc., describes how the client is billed by the THC, based upon the service provided and the number of hours the Temp has worked. The interview process is described in extension 1337, also sponsored by Expertise Temporary Personnel. The recording advises to bring along identification such as a passport, drivers' license, and a social security card. The types of skills required by the industry are outlined, as is general information on the types of questions you need to ask your counselor before accepting a position, such as directions to the job site. Dunhill Temporary Systems of Atlanta, Inc., sponsors extension 1338. This recording deals exclusively with the interview processes. The kinds of skills needed and types of tests available are outlined, including word processing, dictaphone, shorthand, data processing, and technical skills. The caller is advised to be on time and to be confident. We also are reminded that the THC maintains strict standards regarding abilities, personality, and the work ethic.

THCs Across the Country

Different kinds of companies are found throughout the country. For instance, **Anchorage, Alaska** maintains a total of 21 (1994–95):

General Office Support	14
Disabled Persons (General Placement)	1
Inventory/Warehouse	1
Legal Secretarial	1
Seafood Industry (long-term)	1
Technical	3

New Orleans, Louisiana offers 58 (1993–94):

General Office Support	40
Accounting	3
Computer/CAD	1
Design/Industrial/Labor/Technical	8
Hospitality	1
Legal	1
Medical/X-ray	2
Therapists (Mental Health)	1
Transportation/Drivers	1

Like Atlanta, the city of New Orleans also offers tips for Temps through its "Real Consumer Tip" hot-line. To get into the system, dial the main number 504/885–7700, then any of the following extensions: 8335 (How does a Temp Agency work); 8336 (fees); 8337 (information to take to the THC); or 8338 (the interview). As the industry continues to grow, other cities will undoubtedly offer this service.

Sioux Falls, South Dakota is home to 11 THCs (1993–94), which offer a wide variety of services.

Topeka/Shawnee, Kansas claims 12 THCs (1994):

General Office Support	9
Labor	2
Medical	1

and **Butte, Montana** is home to only two, both of which service corporate and industrial clients.

The numbers of specialty THCs placing executives, legal, and medical people are significant, as is the number of THCs that work primarily with skilled and unskilled workers, especially in the South and Midwest. There are also THCs that target seniors, persons with physical challenges, performing artists, gay and lesbian workers, and spouses of military personnel.

The majority of work is for office support, and thus the bulk of ads cater to this segment of the industry. In this spirit, let's look once more at the hypothetical ad we placed in the Introduction:

> Hi $$$—Immed tmp pos avail w/midtwn brkg co. WP skls, dBase & spdsht exp (123), Sten/FLH. Col A+. Fax res attn. Mr. Schlock 555-5555. EOE/M/F/D/V.

We asked before, what are they **really** advertising? Many Temp ads are vague in their descriptions and generally are not for specific positions. By calling for a broad range of skills, THCs are able to attract a wide variety of applicants with diverse capabilities from among whom they can assemble their Temp pools for any situation that may become available. THCs need people with marketable skills such as filing, typing, word processing, spreadsheet analysis, and desktop publishing, to light industrial, architectural, landscaping, and nursing experience.

In responding to the above ad, the novice applicant actually may ask for the person who seemingly placed it. Sometimes this person might even exist! But more often than not, "Mr. Schlock" is a "desk name," a pseudonym designed by the THC to identify you with a specific ad, thus giving them an idea of the kind of assignment you are seeking. The translation of the ad is: "We'll pay you a competitive rate for a temporary position at a brokerage company where you'll be required to do word processing, data entry, and perhaps spreadsheet input. You should have either formal stenography (Gregg or Pittman) or fast long hand because the boss will not draft his or her own memos. We'd prefer someone with a college background, and we are an Equal Opportunity Employer of males, females, disabled individuals, and veterans."

CHAPTER TWELVE

Skills Assessment

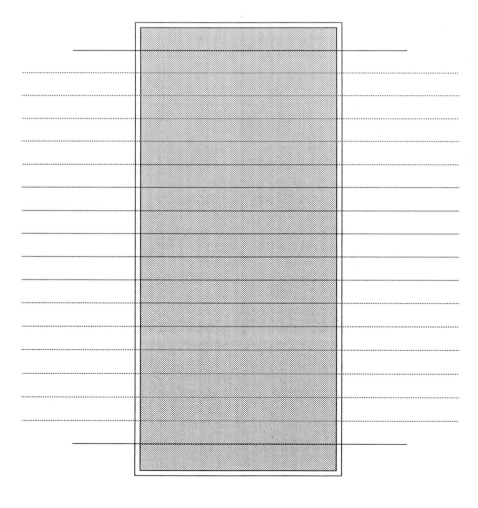

W hat can you do? Legal and medical applicants, architects, gardeners, machinists, technical writers, and other professionals and industry-specific workers have an easier time of answering this question. But if you are a new or re-entrant worker seeking general office, manufacturing, or hospitality assignments, the first thing you need to do is take an inventory of your skills and try to match them to the needs of corporate or industrial America. Make a list of duties and responsibilities at past jobs, or what your education, training, or experience has prepared you for.

Marketable Skills

Perhaps you haven't ever had a regular job. Have you done volunteer work? Have you held an internship? Do you possess good communication skills? Maybe you've typed your own term papers or kept your personal finances on your home computer. Can you drive? Have you worked on an assembly line? Have you balanced a budget? Can you hand out circulars?

Don't toss away anything at this stage as "trivial," "unimportant," or "irrelevant." Once you've compiled a written assessment, decide which skills and experiences are the most marketable. Also, be sure you feel comfortable doing certain kinds of work.

General Office Support

Of course, some skills are more marketable than others. The more current and diverse your skills, the better your chances for securing work. *General office support* THCs expect basic office skills such as a pleasant telephone manner, familiarity with fax and photocopying machines, good clerical skills, and alpha-numeric filing. Typing ability is a plus. You need not be a whiz, but a minimum speed of thirty-five words per minute is required to be considered for a clerk/typist or "receptionist-with-light-typing" job. *Clerical jobs* also call for experience with collating, stuffing envelopes, and perhaps data entry.

Secretarial jobs tend to pay slightly more than clerical positions. They require a faster typing speed and, more often than not, basic word processing. Shorthand (or fast long hand), statistical typing, and dictaphone transcription are advantages.

Administrative assistant positions will almost certainly require word processing expertise. You should type at least fifty-five words per minute and not be terrified of the dictaphone. It's also a good idea to have some familiarity with spreadsheet software. *Executive assistant* positions require all the above, excellent proofreading and editing ability, and knowledge of preparing expense accounts. Unfortunately, the pay differential between administrative and executive assistants is all but nil, although the latter will provide an outlet for sharpening and diversifying your skills.

Other Temp Positions

If you've studied accounting, worked as a bookkeeper, or have experience writing, editing, or proofreading, the THC might be able to place you quicker and at a higher rate. There is also a high demand for bilingual, legal, and medical secretaries, desktop publishers, and graphic designers. Maybe you've had experience with dedicated word processing systems years ago; jobs involving the "dinosaurs" of the computer world are far and few between, but when they do occur you can command an hourly rate nearly twice that of regular word processing secretaries.

Computer-related work is in the highest demand. If you've never touched a computer before in your life but can type, talk with your placement counselor about taking a basic computer orientation class. No one is too old. And no one had worse computerphobia than I! I'll confess, I became comfortable with learning word processing only after playing computer games for more than a year!

Industrial and *Hospitality* positions are more prevalent in small communities. Here, there's a complete gamut of needs to consider including chefs, short-order cooks, punch-pourers, tour guides, draftspersons, custodians, and manufacturers. Persons with licenses and other specialty skills should hook up directly with THCs that cater to their line of work.

How Much Can I Earn?

The increasing need for Temps has dramatically increased the industry's gross revenues, but the expansion of Temps in the pool and the growing number of THCs struggling for their piece of the competition has in some instances **lowered** compensation.

The following **average hourly compensation** listing, extracted from a 1991 NATSS report, appeared in toto in an article in *Purchasing* magazine in August 1992:[3]

Office Clerk	$ 6.35
Receptionist	$ 6.80
Telemarketer	$ 6.85
Data Entry	$ 6.95
Typist	$ 7.00
Bookkeeper	$ 7.05
Machinist	$ 9.45
Secretary	$ 9.85
Word Processor	$ 10.55
Registered Nurse	$ 23.15
Computer Analyst	$ 23.40

The above should be considered a rough guide. Each THC maintains its own compensation structure and takes into account regional median income and spending power factors, the experience of individual Temps, and special arrangements, if any, with individual clients.

To determine if you're getting a fair deal, ask around or simply take the national averages and factor in inflation adjustment and the overall cost of living in your hometown. For instance, some Temp secretaries in major cities (without word processing) earn approximately $11–$12 an hour. It's difficult to find word processing operators who will work for less than $15 an hour. Data entry rates vary nationwide between $10 and $15. Temp physicians, especially those assigned to emergency rooms, earn approximately $60 an hour on the national average, although unlike office support and blue-collar jobs, the figure goes up in rural and economically depressed regions owing to a shortage of primary-care providers (i.e., doctors). Legal secretaries and word processing typists can expect $18 an hour for first shift and as much as $23 an hour for third-shift work in some large cities. Computer programmers command a salary of $40 and up. Talk with people in order to judge for yourself if you indeed are getting a fair deal.

What's Out There?

Most of us will not be temporary oncologists, nuclear physicists, or harpsichordists. It is the corporate or manufacturing environment to-wards which we aim, and our expectations should be as real and as high as our skills allow. The world is changing, and with it the American work force.

A human resources administrator for a large technical operation recently reminded me, "Temps are our future. No question about it. Companies simply cannot afford the health insurance coverage for everyone and the legal battles every time we try to fire someone for incompetence or misconduct, because they try to accuse us of discrimination. So we hire Temps, save money, and ignore the potential legal problems."

We have seen the need for Temps to substitute for full-time employees in corporate, service-sector, medical, legal, technical, manufacturing, and other environments. Temps are also assigned on an indefinite basis in the aftermath of widespread terminations. In addition to white- and blue-collar jobs, there are some unusual tasks that need to be performed as well, as best described by Demaris C. Smith in his *Temporary Employment: The Flexible Alternative:* "Temps have also worked as chicken pluckers, manhole cover watchers, tour guides, escorts . . . Santa Claus, and the Easter Bunny."[4]

By now, the types of positions are apparent. Below is a checklist of the basic "A to Z's" of Temping opportunities.

Temping A to Z

Accounting; Actuarial; Administrative assistant; Architect; Assembly

Banking; Bilingual; Bookkeeping

CAD; Chemistry; Clerical; Collating; Cooking, Custodial

Data Entry; Dental Assistant; Design; Desktop Publishing; Drafting

Editing; Encoding; Executive Consulting

Fax; Filing; Food Services

Gardening; Graphics

Hospitality; Human Resources

IBM® systems; Industry; Inputing; Insurance; Inventory

Janitorial

Keypunch

Lawyer; Legal secretary

Machinist; MacIntosh®; Mailroom; Manufacturing; Medicine; Messenger

Network administration; Nurse

Operations

Paralegal; Phlebotomy; Programmer; Proofreading; Publishing

Quality control

Receptionist; Reporter; Retail

Secretarial; Spreadsheets; Statistical Typist; Stenography; Switchboard; Systems

Technical writing; Telemarketing; Telephones; Translator; Typing

Underwriting; Unix™

Verifications

Waiter; Wang®; Windows; Word processing

X-ray technology; Xerox® machines and memory typewriters

Yet with other skills, you have . . .

Zillions of opportunities!

CHAPTER THIRTEEN

Who Or What Is The THC Looking For?

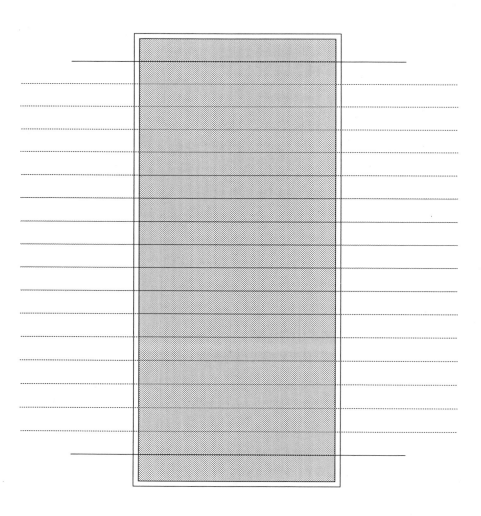

The THC actively seeks to maintain or augment its pool of workers to place in temporary positions. Operating at no cost to the Temp, THCs charge client companies contracted hourly fees and pays their Temps an agreed-upon portion thereof.

THC Goals

The more complex issue concerns whom does the THC consider worthy of its attention. As the primary goal of THCs is securing business, they strive to match Temp applicants to client requisitions. THCs generally know the needs and personalities of their clients so they accept only those applicants they feel can realistically succeed. The prospective Temp must be an asset to the THC's operation. A medical placement service wants only licensed and insured health care practitioners. A legal THC needs proof of having passed the State Bar, paralegal qualifications, and so forth. THCs that traffic mostly in office support staff need persons of all capabilities, from filing to stenography, from loquacious and assertive telemarketers to computer programmers.

THCs desire people who, in their opinion, are emotionally and interpersonally stable enough to represent them. They do not need someone with crumbs in his beard who's wearing a bandanna over hair last shampooed during the Nixon Administration. Placement counselors justifiably shun applicants whose interpersonal manner might be an embarrassment, who dress inappropriately for the work place, whose skills are not up to par, or whose language abilities are unacceptable. They need people who can get the job done, show appropriate sensitivity to their environment, and demonstrate a fitting blend of disinterest in client politics and respect for their business interests. There are, however, still discriminatory policies that occur. We can address them here, although they can much better be dealt with at the Department of Justice.

A Few Words About Discrimination

Like all employers, THCs are subject to the terms and conditions of Title VII of the Civil Rights Act of 1964. As such, they may not deny work to any qualified applicant because of race, creed, religion, and national origin. Today, age, ethnicity, and depending upon local ordinances, sexual orientation are frequently added to the list. A small number of client companies, however, attempt to get away with both subtle and overt forms of discrimination when requisitioning Temps. Suspicious of persons of color, immigrants, seniors, persons with physical challenges, women, unmarried men over thirty, etc., some clients believe they can "special order" a "Single White Female," to borrow a phrase, or whomever else they desire to fit "their image." A responsible THC is one that alerts the client it will not assent to biased requisitions.

Such practices are **infrequent** and when they do occur the perpetrators put themselves in tremendous legal and financial jeopardy. THCs rarely discriminate on their own initiative, provided a person's skills are solid, their manner professional, and their appearance sharp. But despite their best efforts they sometimes do pass on the client's bias, believing themselves a completely innocent bystander. Those few companies that screen Temps for reasons other than assessing their competence are thus engaging in surreptitious but nonetheless illegal discrimination.

In the summer of 1989, the *New York Daily News* ran two stories reporting that two personnel services, both of which maintained a temporary employment division, were overtly discriminating against persons of color.[5] Four new placement counselors related that memos with the innocuous message "See Me" were handed to them during interviews with non-white applicants. "See Me," they later learned was a cryptogram indicating the client had specifically requested a white applicant. The code "AA," for "All American," was also used. The article reported that some counselors took the attitude "You can't make any money if you're going to be that sensitive."

The story was picked up by W–CBS News in August of that year and eventually reached the offices of the Attorney General of the State of New York and the Federal Equal Employment Opportunity Commission. The employment services defended their positions with the naive stance that they were merely fulfilling the wishes of the client. They attempted to make their reasoning sound completely analogous to not assigning an applicant for a position as a security guard to program computers. Nonetheless, the broader interpretation of the law prevailed.

Most of the complaints have since been settled, with penalties such as fines, closures, and damages paid directly to plaintiffs. Similar discriminatory practices were reported that summer in *New York Newsday*.[6] Fortunately, with additional class-action suits pending and stronger antidiscrimination legislation, this kind of behavior is becoming less and less frequent. If, however, you suspect unfair treatment based on race, sex, religion, national origin, disability, sexual orientation, girth, etc., contact your local office of the Equal Employment Opportunity Commission, American Civil Liberties Union, or State Attorney General to register your complaint.

Temps with Physical Challenges

The provisions of the American Disabilities Act of 1992 (ADA) prohibit an employer from inquiring into a job applicant's past or present physical challenges. ADA also forbids discriminating against persons with any such past or present physical challenges. The bill became effective on July 26, 1992 and pertained to businesses with 25 or more employees; businesses with 15 or more employees became subject to the provisions on July 26, 1994.[7]

ADA defines a disabled person as one who has a physical or mental impairment that limits one or more "life activities"; has a record of such an impairment; or is regarded as having such an impairment. It defines a disabled worker as someone who can perform the "essential functions" of a job, with or without reasonable accommodation.

A potential employer may not question an applicant on:

- Medical history
- Prior medical insurance and workers' compensation claims
- Past absenteeism due to illness
- Past treatment for alcoholism and other addictions
- Past treatment for mental illness.

"Reasonable accommodations" mean an employer must:

- Acquire or modify work equipment
- Provide qualified readers or interpreters
- Adjust work schedules
- Make existing facilities, such as restrooms, telephones, and drinking fountains accessible to everyone.

Recent data issued by the President's Commission on Employment of People with Disabilities indicates that the "Disabled Minority" comprises in fact a substantial portion of the American work force. Of course, not all persons who can claim protection under the law are seriously impaired. For example, many arthritis sufferers can take an aspirin to alleviate their symptoms. A hearing loss does not necessarily imply total deafness. Persons with disabilities such as serious sensory loss, epilepsy, missing limbs, or paralysis, however, are a relatively small segment of the total disabled population, and they are the ones who receive the most protection under the law. The President's Commission gives the following statistics:[8]

Hearing impairments	23.3 million
Visual impairments	7.5 million
Speech impairments	2.3 million
Arthritis	30.8 million
Epilepsy	1.2 million
Missing limbs	1.2 million
Partial or complete paralysis	1.4 million
Total:	67.7 million

Finally, the decision by the Equal Employment Opportunity Commission to recognize obesity as a valid disability under ADA, reported in the *Wall Street Journal* on November 12, 1993, clearly indicates ADA allows for a broad interpretation and will certainly be applied to other individuals as well in the near future.[9]

THCs have no authority to insist that clients live up to the requirements of ADA. They cannot demand an employer install wheelchair ramps, special chairs, and so on. However, they can inquire if the client already has ramps or other accommodations for the physically challenged. Few employers will undertake structural modifications for the sole purpose of accommodating Temps because, unlike in the case of full-time employees, they do not receive government incentives such as tax breaks for their efforts. Conversely, many clients are concerned with only employees' abilities, not their disabilities; this is especially true if there are disabled full-time employees already at the firm and facility modification is in place. In any event, persons with physical challenges should not be discouraged from registering with THCs, particularly with those that are experienced in working with disabled persons.

What Else Your Employer Is *Not* Allowed to Ask

Federal antidiscrimination guidelines pertain primarily to issues of race, sex, religion, and disability. But the United States *does not* have written into law a true equal rights amendment guaranteeing equal pay for equal work among the sexes. Philosophical arguments concerning common shower rooms and women Sumo wrestlers aside, an employer reserves the right to pay a male word processing secretary or data entry clerk more than a woman performing the same task, even if she is faster and more efficient, provided that a specific salary figure has not been posted. Often, however, local legislation steps in to rectify inequalities.

The situation is somewhat different in the Temp industry, where THCs maintain rigid compensation structures. The attitude taken by these establishments is, "We pay $13 an hour for word processing secretaries. Male or female. You type seventy-five words a minute and know Multimate™, you get the money, period." And thus the way it should be.

The most strident antidiscrimination legislation in the country is perhaps to be found in New York City. A potential employer, interviewer, recruiter, or any representative of a potential employer, may not ask a job applicant his or her age, marital status, religion, or sexual orientation, nor specifics regarding national origin, race, disabilities, views on or use of birth control, and, surprisingly enough, the name of a person to contact in case of emergency. No queries may be made into the applicant's living situation or the existence of children. Even the subtle forms of such queries are taken into account: An interviewer may not ask a woman if she prefers to be called "Miss," "Mrs.," or "Ms." They may not ask an applicant if he or she was ever arrested, but it is permissible to inquire if the applicant was ever convicted of a felony. In addition, an applicant does not have to furnish any photo ID. However, once a candidate is hired questions concerning age, date of birth, marital status, children, disabilities, preferred form of address, and emergency contact persons can be posed to ensure the employee receives equitable benefits, protection, and respect. For information concerning your locale, contact your local labor department.

Because THCs are employers, they must also play by these rules, but they act with a fundamentally different philosophy. From the time you first walk into the THC, you and your counselor are working with the assumption that you will at sometime in your career be on that THC's payroll, even if for only a day. Therefore, indicating your grandmother or grandchild as an emergency contact saves having to fill out paperwork later on. Answering questions pertaining to dependents up front means facilitating exemptions and withholdings calculations. And unlike a "regular" job interview, photo ID usually is required even before the interview so that all parties can satisfy the I–9 requirements.

In short, you really are not "applying" for a job with the THC, rather, you already are on the books in one fashion or another from the time you register. Thus, a THC interview contains many elements of both an initial interview and a human resources orientation. Whether or not you actually do achieve work assignments remains to be seen. If you find any questions offensive or too personal, end the interview right then and there and report the incident to your state labor department or human rights commissioner.

CHAPTER FOURTEEN

How Does the THC Operate?

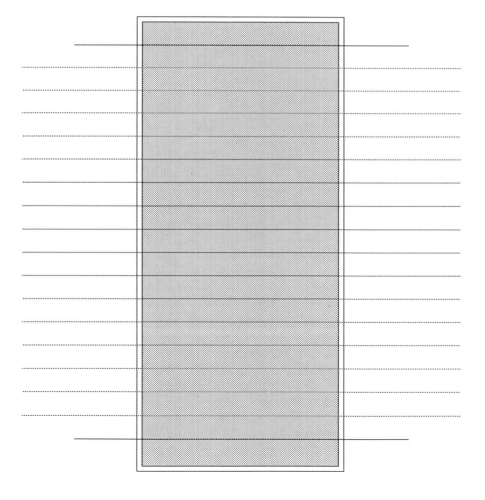

here is no across-the-board flow chart for THC operation, but most THCs utilize a similar scheme. At the head is the executive. In independent THCs, he or she will probably hold the title of president, whereas the owner of a national THC might be styled president or chief executive officer (CEO). Franchises and branches of THCs are headed by managers, regional directors, or vice presidents. You probably will have little or no direct contact with the executive, again depending upon the size and set-up of the operation.

Organization

Reporting to the executive are the placement director, financial officer, and marketing director. The financial unit controls the billing and receivables of clients, expenditures, taxes, and salaries for regular staff and the Temps. The marketing staff and account reps, often one in the same, generate and maintain business. They are the ones who target and solicit clients by direct mailing, telephone calls, visits, and power lunches. Because most clients are not exclusive and constantly shop around for new THCs or try to renegotiate pre-existing contracts, marketing people and account reps work long hours promoting and selling their product, which, in a sense, is you.

Once a relationship is established with a client, the placement coordinator is made aware of the terms of the contract, which he or she passes on to the appropriate placement counselor, whose job is to secure an available Temp, confirm the order and hourly charges, and send the Temp to the job site. Counselors often work on a partial salary, partial commission basis. This is an integral factor in the Counselor-Temp relationship, because counselors will only procure work for people they feel can best represent the interests of the THC.

Placement counselors should never be thought of as "a friend," no matter how long you have worked for them. The counselor's relationship with you extends for only as long as you continue to prove your ability, diplomacy, and potential to generate revenue for the THC. Remember that counselors work with hundreds of Temps and sometimes have to make spur-of-the-moment decisions in which all avouched loyalties are seemingly disregarded. But this is an unfair rap, and the vast majority of placement counselors genuinely enjoy finding work for people.

The counselor is your boss. It is he or she who matches Temps to client requisitions. Because requisitions must be filled immediately, the counselor may assign a Temp already on the premises (someone on "stand-by," in the waiting room and ready to be sent out immediately).

If no one is on stand-by, the counselor will call Temps at home to find out who is available for work and how fast they can get there. If you want to work on any given day but don't want the hassle of stand-by, notify your counselor the afternoon prior or call by 8:30 A.M., dressed and ready to go.

What the Client Expects

The client company may request a Temp to substitute for a full-time employee who is absent, to assist with a specific task for which they have had to augment their staff for a defined period, to serve as an interim employee while they conduct a search for a full-time person, or to act as a surrogate employee for a position that will never be approved for a full-time slot. In the first instance, there will be a specific hierarchy ("You will be working for Mr. Rottenburg while his secretary is trying to post bail," or "Report to Mr. Fiocco, Ms. Kerkhoven, and Mr. Ginsberg, answering phones and typing memos"). There will also be a particular "seat," "desk," or "station" to which you will be assigned. The belongings of the person for whom you are substituting will undoubtedly be there (e.g., "work shoes," pictures of the kids), and you might find specific instructions regarding telephones, faxes, file location, and procedures left by that person.

In the second instance, you might be escorted to a work area. If the project in question is large, the client may have brought in other Temps, perhaps from several THCs. The client may also provide a work coordinator to explain the project and demonstrate the tasks. An assembly-line type of work-flow might be devised, or the Temps might work independently, each processing data from the same "in-box." Large corporations need only a working cog in their wheel of business, while smaller operations or divisions need a good team player.

A responsive, insightful client is one that adheres to the following guidelines:[10]

1. Specifies what the job entails and the expectations of the Temp's qualifications and experience;

2. Does not overload the Temp with information concerning the company's personnel and procedures;

3. Makes the Temp comfortable with the environment; and

4. Gives experienced Temps some degree of leeway.

The client company expects and pays for a Temp who can:

1. Meet their expectations;
2. Cause no interruption in work-flow or profitability; and
3. Arouse, beget, cause, defend, encourage, generate, hearten, initiate, justify, kindle, license, manage, nurture, originate, provoke, quicken, rile, trigger, undertake, vindicate, warrant, or be the center of *no* attention, negative or otherwise, or any interpersonal conflict whatsoever.

In short, the client is counting on the THC to provide what they need. They work with nationally-known THCs because of their reputation for carefully testing and screening applicants, and they contract with small, localized THCs in the hope of securing lower fees and dedicated service. They often negotiate volume discounts, and they take into consideration the proximity of the THCs they select.[11]

It is your responsibility to assess the situation at hand and proceed accordingly, bearing in mind that the client's satisfaction will increase business for the THC and land you more job assignments, whereas their disappointment will impact negatively on the THC's balance sheet and also affect you.

Registering and Interviewing

Registering with three or four THCs affords exposure to a large pool of job possibilities. Chances are you will work primarily for only one or two, but it is always a good idea to have your skills on file at several, especially during slow seasons. Also, the more THCs willing to work with you, the more competitive you become.

Some THCs will see you only by appointment, although the trend in most cities is to "walk-in." If in doubt, check the THC ads in the newspaper or call. Telephone queries should be brief. Just say something like, "Hello, I saw your ad in the newspaper (or the phone book, or whatever) and would like to set up an appointment to register with your company."

If you opt for a "walk-in," don't come with the Help Wanted section in your hands and a pen clenched between your teeth. There is no greater turn-off. Show respect and you'll get respect. Bury the newspaper in your bag or use a small, concealed pad for your hit list. Dress in a corporate mode but not as if you are chairing the Board of Directors. Ten years ago it was acceptable to dress casually at the registration interview, with the understanding that appropriate attire would be donned when you were sent out on a job. Today, with the advent of professional men and women entering the Temp scene, that's all changed. Appearance is important (see Chapter 15, "What to Wear").

While appointments can be scheduled at any time, the best days for unsolicited THC hopping are Tuesday, Wednesday, and Thursday. Try to drop in between 10:00 A.M. and 2:30 P.M. otherwise you'll find yourself in the middle of rush hour, when the counselors are sending out and checking up on the day's orders or filling afternoon requisitions. Also, realize that the registration processes takes approximately an hour and a half, so allow adequate time for each appointment.

The first person you will meet at the THC is the receptionist. Be cheerful and polite. He or she sees dozens of people every day so you've got to try to show you're special. Say good morning or good afternoon, and state you'd like to register with the THC, just in case there was any doubt whatsoever.

The receptionist will ask for your name and inquire as to what kind of work you are seeking. Proof of citizenship or a copy of a work permit will be requested. The documents will be photocopied and filed. For American citizens, a U.S. passport is the best form of identification. You can also use a social security card in conjunction with some other form of ID such as a birth certificate, drivers' license, or college or military ID. Other persons eligible to work in the United States should bring their work permit in addition to other photo ID. At most THCs, failure to produce proof of citizenship or a work permit ends the registration process then and there. Don't get offended and say, as I once heard a woman admonish, "You're making a big mistake losing such a good worker." Since the signing on November 6, 1986 of the Immigration Reform and Control Act of 1986 (S.1200—Public Law 99–603), all employers are **legally bound** to hire only American citizens or persons with valid work permits.

At this point you most likely will be handed a clipboard with an application, questionnaire, and Forms I–9 (eligibility to work) and W–4 (tax withholdings). You might also receive a written or verbal rundown on the THC. Always thank the receptionist. Don't fill out the application at the desk. Move to the waiting area, answer every question to the best of your ability, then hand back the documents and clipboard.

Be both honest and prudent in filling out the application. For example, if you have multiple university degrees and couldn't find a job as a Sanskrit translator, put down only what you think is relevant for landing a Temp assignment. If you've got business or professional experience or degrees, make sure you indicate so. Persons registering with specialty THCs or consulting firms might bring a reduced photocopy of a diploma, a practitioner's license, or a more detailed *curriculum vitae* (C.V.) that includes training, place(s) of internship, publications, and/or specific projects completed.

Applications vary from THC to THC, but format and content are similar. As stated in Chapter 13, the Temp application might go beyond what is considered proper questioning of a potential employee, because the understood contract between you the THC is different than in a full-time situation. The application will ask for your name, permanent and mailing address(es), time window available for work, educational background, skills, type of work you are seeking, and information regarding previous employment. You might also be asked if you have any physical challenges, if you've ever been convicted of a felony, your veteran status, and your eligibility to be bonded. Temp applicants are sometimes asked to furnish references, which probably will be contacted by the THC, but never by the client. Clients, however, reserve the right to fingerprint, run FBI checks, and test for drugs.

THCs are required by law to follow the guidelines of the 1964 Civil Rights Act and all Federal immigration laws.

Skills questions must also be answered as honestly as possible. If you boast a typing speed of 135 words per minute, you will be compelled to prove it. Your B+ in French 201 earned in your sophomore year at Erasmus Hall High School in 1953 is of no interest to your counselor. But if you are truly bilingual, i.e., able to read, write, speak, and think in a foreign language with the same or greater fluency as in English, make a point of indicating your ability on the application and discuss the possibilities for bilingual work with the counselor during the ensuing interview. If your non-English reading and writing skills are as good as your spoken ability, you might be able to secure work as a translator or interpreter, which can earn you at least $25 an hour. You should also make it known if you have experience in customer service, insurance underwriting, dedicated word processing systems such as Wang® and

DisplayWriter™ or any of the dinosaurs like AM 425™, Linear™, Micom™, Savin™, or Vydec™. This shows you've been around for a while and many of these skills will earn you a high premium.

The receptionist or exam administrator may brief you on the tests. Persons seeking office work will be given a basic clerical skills test to determine if they are functionally literate. Don't scoff at the idea of being asked to circle which of the following is correct:

Callege   Colledge   College   Collige

Remember, you might have a master's degree from Harvard and a medical degree from Oxford, but the THC is concerned only with ranking you against other Temps, some of whom might feel confident with choosing the spelling with the "D."

Most THCs will offer you the option of taking specialized tests. Select whichever you feel will benefit you. There are several kinds of tests including accounting/bookkeeping, typing, shorthand, and word processing. There are translations to be done in French, Spanish, German, and Russian, among other languages. There are multiple choice and "fill-in" exams in the nursing and civil engineering fields, and there are sample computer programs to be written.

Always ask to do a practice run. The typewriter keyboard might be different from what you're used to, or the eraser key might have been disabled. Word processing tests are more complicated. In the old days, i.e., before 1990, word processing tests were similar to typing tests, although the copy would include some underlining, bolding, paragraph indents, and super- and subscripting. Nowadays, the tests themselves often come on interactive software.

There is also the possibility the test will take the form of a multiple choice or "fill-in" exam rather than a "hands-on." This may include questions such as "Which keystrokes are required to change the top-bottom margins in WordPerfect™ 5.1?" The best way to prepare for this kind of exam is to memorize the template or even the "Quick Help" section of various software manuals. Interactive testing is becoming the norm, despite all its problems. THCs think highly of them and even advertise their use to potential clients in the trade magazines.

It is not uncommon for the test scores to be analyzed by the receptionist who will then notify the appropriate counselor (clerical/typist, accounting, word processing, specialty skills, etc.) that you are ready for the interview.

CHAPTER FIFTEEN

The Interview

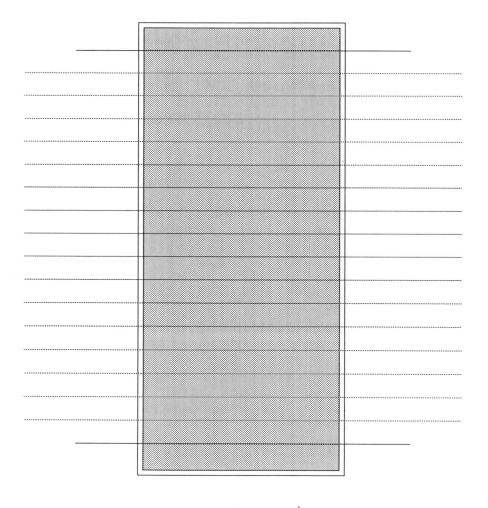

Preparing for the Interview

The purpose of the interview is to enable counselors to assess your appearance and interpersonal skills so they can determine if they can feel comfortable placing you out in the field. Bearing this in mind, you must prepare to sell yourself.

Getting Psyched

Your skills, dress, communicative style, and reasons and availability for Temping should convey the basic subtext, "I am a good investment. I am worth your time, will bring in commissions, and will safeguard and even enrich your relationship with your clients. Take advantage of what I've got to offer." Convey this by your responsible appearance, professional style, and skills.

What to Bring

Some Temps bring résumés to their initial THC interviews. In the past, résumés were not necessary, but some THCs now like to have a look at them. Lawyers, physicians, architects, technical writers, and persons seeking contingent executive positions should bring a detailed C.V. Technical and "ghost" writers should bring along a list of publications and two or three samples of their work. Come prepared with a legal pad, two ballpoint pens, and proof of citizenship or work permit.

What to Wear

Owing to the recent conservative bent of the industry, casual clothing is no longer acceptable at Temp interviews. Don attire proper for a corporate or industrial environment. Your clothing should not reveal the "inner you," rather, it must reflect the responsible you, the you that will fit in downtown or any other place. Wear what is appropriate for **an employee of the THC,** not that of "just a Temp." This is NOT discrimination. The THC has every right to protect its interests, and a dress code, written or otherwise, stands. Your counselor will advise you of any particular dress code required for a specific assignment, as he or she is well-aware that you can always dress down later on.

Wear what you look best in. True, some of us look best in motorcycle leathers, but if you've opted to play the work game the rules need to be followed. There can be some relaxation of the precepts later on, but for now think only of getting your foot in the door and the feel of that first paycheck. Actual on-the-job apparel may differ from first-day dress once you get a better idea of the assignment.

Full-time employees tend to follow a simple maxim: the lower down on the ladder you are, the less formal you may dress. Thus the quip, "mailroom and clerical people don't change shoes." The antipode is: persons seeking promotions should dress as if they already have attained the next level or rung of the said ladder.

Women aiming for word processing pools and administrative assistant positions should wear suits at the interview and on the first day of an assignment until told otherwise. Receptionist and clerical positions generally call for a solid-colored skirt and a matching jacket. Women of a more mature age often wear low-keyed floral patterns. Most fabrics are acceptable, with the exception of 100% polyester (inelegant) and velvet (too formal). Similarly, full-length dresses are not recommended for the reason. Colors should reflect the season. Wear stockings and comfortable shoes, but avoid high heels.

Make-up is a personal choice (for women and men, although "bronzers," hair coloring, and $30-a-session tans are becoming somewhat dated), but use discretion. Less is better. You might want to have your nails trimmed neatly and manicured. Nail polish for women may be clear or a basic red or pink. Avoid purple, green, yellow, blue, and black, as well as gaudy designs. Also your hair should be neat and clean. It should not add eight inches to your height.

Women can wear up to three pieces of jewelry, in addition to earrings, a wedding or engagement ring, or a watch. Again, leave the "real you" at home. Keep religious ornaments tucked in, earrings should not hang below your jaw bone, only one necklace (gold, silver, mixed, or string of pearls) and bracelet, and no more than three rings. And **never** chew gum or smoke at the interview or while working at an assignment.

Men should come to the interview wearing dress slacks, shirt and tie, and a jacket. If seeking specialty or consulting work, wear a suit reflecting the season. Don't wear garish colors or patterns. Ties may be solid, striped, or paisley; abstain from "gimmick" ties. Students and collegiate and artistic types should refrain from wearing the corduroy slacks, white turtle neck, and tweed-with-elbow-patches ensemble associated with academics. If you decide against the suit jacket or blue blazer for the interview, at least wear a long-sleeved button-down dress shirt and a stylish tie. Belts are more appropriate than the more formidable suspenders. Also, don't wear religious medals, bracelets, earrings, or political and/or humorous buttons. The exception to any of the above, however, is for persons seeking manufacturing, light clerical, messenger, or mailroom positions, in which case casual slacks, such as corduroy, and a shirt and tie is entirely appropriate.

Finally, if you are unsure of what to wear conduct "field research" by going down to the financial or downtown district of the nearest city and observe what people in your age group are wearing. Take mental notes and decide for yourself what clothing makes the wearer command respect without appearing ostentatious. You needn't spend hundreds of dollars on an interview outfit, but do expect to make an investment of approximately $75–$100 for women, $125–$200 for men, in addition to shoes.

The point of all this is to **sell yourself** to the THC. And once they "sell," or more correctly, "rent" you to a client, you can adjust your appearance accordingly.

The Interview

THCs placing mainly office support Temps will interview you if you dress appropriately, demonstrate functional literacy, and show proper identification. But it's not a guarantee you'll be first on the list for every position that comes up. Counselors interview dozens of people every day, especially during the summer months or after a massive downsizing has occurred in their city or town. You have got to impart you're not just another desperate person who has walked in off the street. You have researched the market and this particular THC is the one you have chosen to work with. This you can make clear by assuming a confident and professional approach and appearance. Stand (or sit) straight, smile, and have confidence in yourself. By giving the impression you are well-seasoned at this, the THC staff will take notice of you.

General office support, manufacturing, and medical THCs will most likely interview you after your initial registration is complete. Consulting firms might schedule an interview for a day or two afterwards so they can have enough time to fully evaluate your skills and perhaps check on your references.

Shortly after the receptionist notifies the placement department that you're ready for the interview, a counselor will come out to meet you. Shake hands if one is extended to you. Return nod for nod and smile for smile. And remember that human resources people are terminally upbeat. That's their job. Because of the magnitude of people they have to deal with every day in person and on the phone, the significance of each and every contact, and the responsibility for bringing in and maintaining business, they sometimes appear to be superficial. However, keeping their own interests in mind, a good counselor knows a good catch when he or she sees it.

The counselor will be looking you over while reviewing your scores and application. Chief among the things they look for are,

Is the applicant:

- Neat and clean?
- Dressed for success?
- Articulate?
- Cordial?
- A corporate type?
- A good, productive worker?

Also,

- Can I trust him/her on the job-site?
- Are his/her thoughts organized?
- Does this person have a "real" life?
- Can this person follow instructions?
- Can he/she handle stressful situations? and
- Is this person a good investment for the company?

Answer these questions yourself. Be critical and objective. You should be your harshest judge, and if you pass that test, you will pass the interview with flying colors.

Temp interviews are usually brief owing to the time constraints imposed by the sheer bulk of applicants and the number of positions counselors fill every day. The counselor might ask you how you happened to come to that particular THC. If you were referred by a friend, mention that person's name only if he or she is in a good light. If your friend is still working for the THC, they might receive a referral bonus. Make the counselor feel his or her company is the best for you.

A savvy counselor can complete the interview within ten minutes. Assuming you are suitably dressed, groomed, and coherent, the counselor will first consider your test scores. If he or she is confident you can fit into one or more of their work classifications, little additional information is needed. Essentially, the counselor is concerned with your appearance, availability, aptitude for learning new procedures, and interpersonal style, namely, that you can work with and for different types of people without requiring a period of adjustment beyond the initial greeting.

The counselor might be curious about your reasons for Temping but may not have to ask you directly. If you are between age 18 and 28 and say you can only work from June 15th until August 15th, they have already figured out you are a college student. If you are in your 30s or 40s and mention managerial, technical, or manufacturing and assembly experience, they may peg you as a casualty of a downsizing, merger, or bankruptcy. Seniors are apparently retirees or perhaps recent widows or widowers in need of extra income.

If the question arises, explain succinctly and in the most positive light. If you've been laid off, you might indicate you have left your job as a widget maker to spend more time with your family. Another good answer is that you are not really in a position to commit to a "full-time" job until six months from now. You can also intimate that you've got an alternative agenda ("I'm a writer/musician/actress, and . . ."), because the counselor will interpret the subtext as "I'm bright, creative, living in this city permanently, and will Temp for you for the rest of my life, so I'm a good catch."

Give some parameters as to your availability. The longer you are available for work, the greater the interest the counselor will take in you. Don't show any financial desperation; rather, act confident. Show them that you have worlds to offer and that the THC is making a wise investment in procuring work for you.

It's generally fruitless to bargain for hourly rates at this point. But do come with some idea of the going rates for your particular skills and work with that. If you are used to earning $15 an hour, you might have to settle for $14 or even $13 when starting with a new THC. You undoubtedly will aim to increase that after a few successful assignments, or leave that THC. Educational background rarely affects salary level, with the notable exception of the specialty fields (legal, medical, computers, etc.).

As the interview winds down, the counselor may brief you on the workings of the THC and the kinds of jobs and approximate hourly wage they will try to obtain for you. This is a good indication that you've been accepted for their pool. Counselors often talk to Temp applicants as if they've been hired, and in a sense, most will be.

Once this has been established, the counselor will close the interview by giving you his or her card, some blank timesheets, and perhaps a brochure that outlines company policies, dress codes, and expectations.

The counselor will remind you one more time that you work for them, not the client. Don't examine the handouts until you're out the door. Being given a timesheet and direct phone number does not guarantee that work will materialize, but you're well on your way.

The Aftermath

After a full day of registering with THCs, you still have much to do. If you want work for the next day, start making your phone calls around 3:00 P.M. Call from a pay phone if you're still on the road. If you have not yet been assigned, ask the counselors when you should call back.

If possible, invest in an answering machine that allows you to pick up your messages when you're out. Keep your message brief and avoid ones like, "This is Sinbad, I've already travelled six seas and I'm about to embark on the seventh, so . . ." Counselors are professionals and don't have time for cute or whimsical messages. Make their job easier and they'll be grateful.

In slow seasons it might take a few days for your first assignment to come through. There might be something available for you, but at a lower job classification. If nothing else comes in, you should accept that position so that your counselor can see you are indeed serious about working. Your counselor might also have offered you a lower job grade just to see how you operate in the field before placing you in a higher paying position.

> Finally, remember to pat yourself on the back. You've taken a major step in getting your foot in the door at the work place. You've done something to be very proud of.

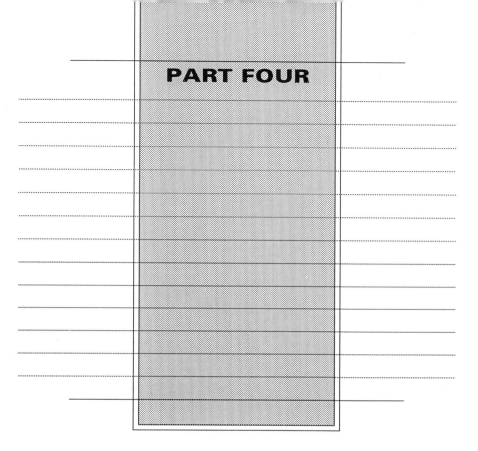

PART FOUR

Now That You're Working . . .

CHAPTER SIXTEEN

Bingo: You've Got The Assignment!

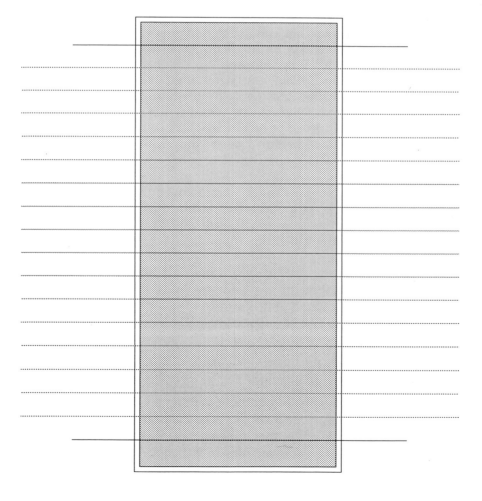

ypically, one endures a miss or two before a hit. Don't panic if the first few calls to the THC are unsuccessful. Call the counselors back in the afternoon. If you haven't been assigned by closing time, start over again early the next morning. When you call, make sure you're ready to be at a potential job site by 9:00 A.M. You might also be asked to come in on stand-by, which greatly increases your chances of getting an assignment that day.

On Call

Every now and then I'll get a call from the THC at 5:00 P.M. or shortly after because an emergency one- or two-day assignment has come up. In some cities, it's not uncommon for applicants who have indicated they will accept night work to get a call around midnight telling them to hop into a taxi and get right over to the client. Some communities boast one or more of the famous "Temp Houses," apartments habitually occupied by "Generation X'ers." The roommates are usually energetic young people, often recent graduates or performing artists pursuing creative and alternative agendas, who register together at THCs. All have excellent administrative and word processing skills in addition to their individual capabilities. The counselors know all the members of the household and can rely on the availability of one or more of them at the drop of a hat.

When you call your THC in the afternoon and work is available for the next day, the conversation will resemble the one I generally have with my favorite counselor, to whom I shall refer as Sarah. The dialogue typically goes something like this:

> L: Hey, Sarah, Lewis B. here. I'm just letting you know I'm available for work for the next three weeks. First or second shift's okay.
>
> S: Hi, Lewis. I'm working on something for you. I forgot, do you do Lotus™?
>
> L: Yes. But I'd prefer WordPerfect™, if possible. What do you have available?
>
> S: It's a one-week assignment at Penguin City Tuxedo Corp. They need a secretary to the president. Go to 347 17th Avenue, 13th floor, and ask for Mr. Chumley Livingston. Hours are nine to five-thirty minus forty

minutes for lunch. WordPerfect™, some Lotus™, heavy phones. Dress corporate. If you have a tux or a black suit wear it, if not, anything dark. And you need a black bow tie. They'll lend you one if you don't own one.

L: Sounds great. 347 17th. 13th floor. What's that near?

S: Between Zeeland and Yukon Streets. Take the K train to Admiral Byrd Station. It's only three blocks from there. And call me as soon as you get settled.

L: Okay, Sarah. I'm up to it. What's the rate?

S: $16 an hour.

L: Sounds good. Anything else I need to know?

S: Yes, bring along a sweater. They said it gets chilly in that building. And call me! Bye.

In this brief encounter we learn that the position is secretary to the top man. Word processing and spreadsheets are involved, and there will be a lot of phones ringing. Since it's a fashion company and the assignment is in the executive wing, it's imperative to honor the company's dress code. The hours, lunch policy, and compensation were clear.

Accurate, easy-to-follow directions are paramount to any Temp assignment. Urban centers are easier to discern because of mass transit. If cars are involved, it is the counselor's responsibility to procure detailed instructions for you, using the most accessible roads and plenty of landmarks. Inquire about parking. Consultants and freelancers may want to consider purchasing personal fax machines so they can have maps and contracts sent over instantly. Owing to the apparent use of this equipment for business purposes, the costs often may be written off at tax time.

CHAPTER SEVENTEEN

The First Day

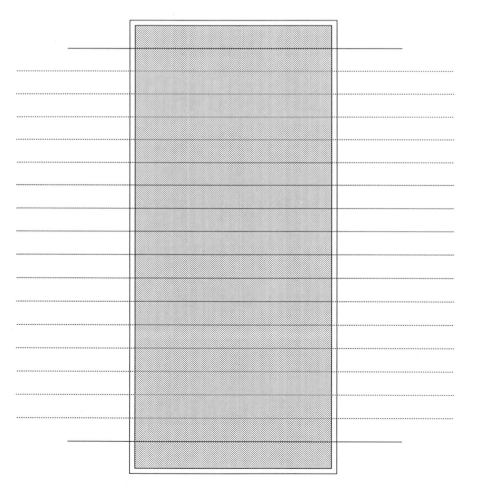

I t's only normal to feel apprehensive about a new assignment even though we Temps are mavens at being transient. Some people take "first day syndrome" in stride; others experience minor panic; a few actually enjoying moving around every couple of days or weeks. It's not only different companies, but different locations as well. And of course, different people and personalities.

At the Job

So, you've found the address. If there's a security station, give the guard your name, the THC's name, the name of the person you're going to see, and the phone extension, if you have it. Bank headquarters might send you to the security office to be fingerprinted. Fear not. Unless you're an escaped felon, no federal marshals are waiting to take you away. Ideally, your counselor will warn you beforehand. If you were not advised, the choice to continue is up to you.

I once overheard a counselor on the phone with a Temp who refused to be fingerprinted. The young woman had been escorted out of the building after squabbling with a security officer, who she said was "rude." Trying to contain her anger, the counselor explained it was just a formality and she would never have to see the officer again because she'd be working in a different building, with "nice" people. This was to no avail. I was silently fuming at this person for turning down a $15-a-hour spot during a particularly bad summer, when I had worked only four days in the past two weeks. Needless to say, she never again was called by that THC. In most cases you will not be fingerprinted—I've only had two assignments that required it and was forewarned both times.

Once you've made it into the elevator, your first stop will probably be Human Resources, if the company is large, or the main reception area. The receptionist or human resources representative will give you a temporary badge and instruct you as to where to go. Don't walk in holding your coffee and doughnut for all the world to see. Proceed directly to your assigned area. There might be a receptionist on the floor or a security door and a phone receiver. If the latter, dial the extension and tell them you're here.

A very cheery, nicely dressed young woman was at the other end of one such call I made. She came to the door, a burst of energy. She grabbed my hand and said, "Hi, Lewis, I'm SO GLAD you're here. Don't scream when you see the desk, we haven't had a secretary in over a week!"

I'm not an archeologist, but I nonetheless assessed that the work area required careful excavation. She showed me the coffee machine, demonstrated the telephone, then turned on the computer. "I'm computer illiterate," she said. We managed to get on the LAN so I could at least get started. I still hadn't a clue what she did, so I asked if she was also a secretary. Big mistake. Turned out she was divisional vice president. My lesson from that is assume *nada*. Just ask, "What is your position in the company?"

You can ask your Temp boss about restrooms and lunch hours. If the mysteries of the coffee machine are not revealed to you at that time, ask a secretary or receptionist a little later. **Do** ask about telephones as soon as you're ready to start working. The first and ideally only personal phone call you should make is to the THC to let your counselor know you've made it in on time.

First days range from the dull to the exhilarating, from the pleasant to the horrendous. If a job seems to be an immediate disaster, don't run for the hills. Give it another day or two, or maybe a week. You might not know where anything is, but don't bother the chairman of the board for help with locating files. Ask other secretaries or clerical staff for help.

Technical freelancers, legal consultants, and Temps in medicine, pharmaceuticals, nursing, and laboratory environments will undoubtedly receive a detailed briefing and meet all the parties with whom they'll be working. The environment will be more structured and at the same time less formal, as most people will be on an equal footing in terms of educational degrees and backgrounds. Manufacturing people will be shown the ropes as soon as they arrive at the job site.

Office Equipment

Phones

You need to know only two things about telephones, namely, when to use them and when not to. Both rules are simple: use the telephones for (the client's) business purposes **only** and the other falls into place. Phones are routinely monitored by recording devices or computerized timers that log the numbers and the amount of time spent on each call made or received.

Always ask how to operate the phones. Dialing out might require pressing 0, 1, 9, or something like 88, and conferencing and transferring differs from system to system. If you are answering several different lines, keep everyone's name (first and last) and extension close by until you memorize the list. Ask if they prefer the phone to be answered before the second ring, if they want their calls screened, and if they want to be interrupted and for whom. Above all, use your best phone manners.

Fax and Photocopy Machines

Once you are shown where the equipment is located and given the required keycard or codes, if needed, use the machines only for the purpose for which they were meant, namely, company business. Don't fax your résumé or photocopy your latest manuscript. If you simply cannot resist the temptation to do so, try asking for permission. If denied, it is a personal choice to risk dismissal just to save a few dollars. The same holds true for binding machines, printers, and so forth.

I've seen my share of altercations at photocopy machines. There are the "I just have one page to do" types—they never tell you they need 647 copies of that **one** page—and there's always someone copying dozens of receipts, laying out each and every one manually. Then there's the executive assistant who feels he or she takes priority over everyone else. Go with the flow, but at the same time hold your ground. If you run into difficulties don't quibble, alert your manager instead. But again, the general rule prevails: be polite and considerate of others, and they most likely will return the favor.

Don't be surprised if a manager tells you to hide everything at the photocopy or fax machine lest someone will get wind of what the boss is up to. Whatever thoughts you might have about paranoia, it is always a good idea to keep your documents under your nose, rather than someone else's, and not to discuss any of the contents therein.

CHAPTER EIGHTEEN

Budgeting Your Time

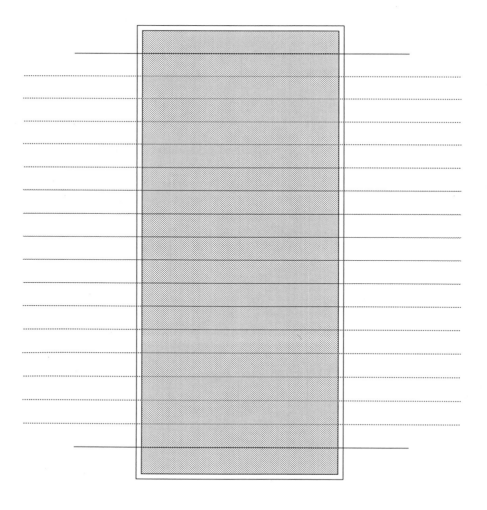

Temps working in the manufacturing sector will find a structured routine at almost all their assignments. The same kind of environment awaits office support Temps sent to assist with special projects, especially data entry, which tends to operate on an "assembly-line" principle. In other words, work-flow is steady and constant, and the pace will vary little during the course of the day.

Pacing Yourself

Temps working in the technical, legal, and the medical and scientific domains often will be part of a group and work accordingly, while technical writers and architects generally have more leeway to pace themselves as long as they meet the deadlines. Most people find the day goes faster when the work-flow is constant. I've frequently been told something like, "I was doing a project and then I looked at my watch and saw what time it was. I couldn't believe it was already my lunch hour."

There is no regular formula for clerical, secretarial, and word processing situations. Some clerical settings resemble an assembly line. Typically, there will be an in-box or a work coordinator to allocate tasks. For instance, there might be forms to process before being sent over to the data entry department. One such assignment I had involved collating thousands of multipart forms, sending the "yellows" to accounting, the "greens" to MIS, the "blues" to legal, and the "originals" to central files. I shudder to think how many Temps were needed in the file room.

Other times you will have busy hours or days and some rather insipid intervals of boredom. Since you really have no idea of what to expect from a particular assignment, bring along a newspaper and perhaps a paperback book to read just in case there is substantial down-time. But be discreet. Maybe you can do some "self-starter" tasks, which will make your manager take notice of your initiative, as well as alleviate the boredom.

Some managers will be up front about periodic work shortages and indicate you may discreetly read. Others might suggest you read client literature, just in case their bosses are in the area. You can also write letters or work on your novel or whatever on the computer, but **under no circumstances** should you save anything personal on the hard drive or network drive. When you save, save only to a floppy disk. This is because computer systems, like the telephones, are routinely monitored and any non-work-related files may be dumped. In addition, if you're suddenly dismissed from an assignment you'll have no way of retrieving your work.

Work-flow can be a problem when you are overburdened. If you work for only one or two people in a high traffic setting you should be able to negotiate a schedule. However, when several people are involved, everyone undoubtedly will want his/her work done first. If they cannot sort things out, ask the office manager for assistance. If there's no office manager or anyone else who can moderate, ask the seniormost person for advice on organizing a work-flow. If you are going to be at that particular assignment for only a few days it probably will not be worth your time. If, however, the job will exceed a week, attempt some intervention. You can ask if outside correspondence is to be done before internal memos, graphics before data entry, and so forth. If you do not get any cooperation and feel completely buried in paperwork and other tasks, ask your THC to arbitrate a work-flow.

Keeping Busy

A "Catch-22" frequently encountered is a deficiency of work and the unwillingness of client company managers to permit you to do anything other than stare at the walls. These are the same people who sternly tell you to "look busy."

Among the "self-starter" projects, you can format floppy disks. Or, with permission, reorganize the computer files into subdirectories. You might tidy up the desk or arrange the paper files. Your manager might also be able to procure some work for you from another person or department.

Then there are those times when there is absolutely nothing for you to do but wonder why you were sent there in the first place. Luckily, this is not the norm, indeed, it has become quite rare these days. Six years ago I accepted a succession of one-day assignments at a major investment company. Classified as a word processing secretary, I was told I would only be answering phones and perhaps make a few photocopies, two or three times a day. I succeeded in answering no more than four phone calls during the course of any given day because the other secretaries beat me to it. The question in my mind was why pay someone at a word processing rate just to do this. One of the full-time secretaries finally explained that company policy required every desk with a computer to be staffed by someone who could word process. Somehow, I was not surprised when this company was acquired three years after and its personnel was scaled down to a bare skeleton.

More recently, I worked at a high-energy, growing business in the fashion district. I served as an interim administrative assistant for a senior marketing agent while the company interviewed applicants for the full-time position. She gave me a good run-down of the operation and trained me on the Company's internal databases. The desk was heavy-traffic, but the different tasks made the day go by quickly.

One morning, the boss called the office at a quarter past nine to say she was detained at a meeting and wouldn't be in until half past eleven. I asked another manager if I could help her. She told me to wait at my desk for another twenty minutes. I poured myself a cup of coffee, returned to my desk, and started reading the newspaper. Another woman came charging down the hall, strutted up to me arms akimbo, reached forward, abruptly closed my paper and snapped, "Please don't ever do that here again." Then she walked off. I started writing letters on the computer until the twenty minutes had passed. I returned to the other manager, who finally gave me some inventory control work to do.

It truly is awkward to find yourself regarded a robot who can be turned on and off at someone else's whim. No one should make you feel as if it's your fault that there are gaps in work-flow. It is entirely the company's responsibility. You can expect some moments of bore-dom, but should you prefer to do company work, which after all you are being paid for, ask around.

CHAPTER NINETEEN

Some Practical Advice

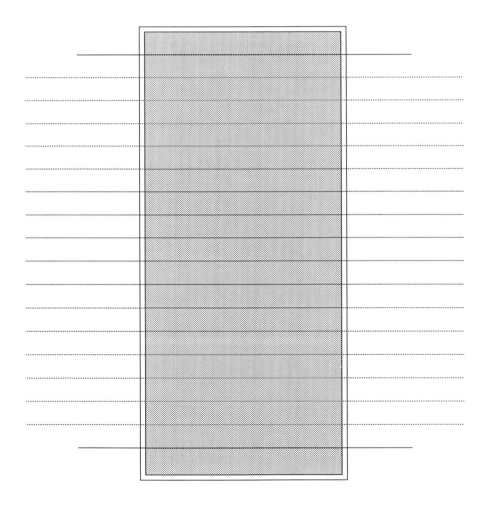

Temps are professional people, and they work for professional people. A few common courtesies will greatly enhance your working relationship with your THC. The following should be made part of your regular routine.

- Always call your counselor when you arrive at a new job site. This lets them know you've arrived on time and are settled in. Give the counselor a phone number where you can be reached.

- If an emergency comes up and you're going to be late or need the day off, notify your THC. If you know the night before, speak with the evening placement counselor or leave a message on the THC's answering machine. **Do not** deal directly with your temporary supervisor unless you've been at the assignment for a while and feel comfortable with him/her. Your counselor should be the first person to know so someone else can be assigned.

- Check in with your counselor once a week, even if the assignment is long-term. Let the THC know if you're enjoying the assignment and if everything is going smoothly.

- Notify your counselor if an assignment is coming to an end and you will not be available for work the following day. Give some idea as to when you'll be available again.

- Always ask your counselor to update your file whenever you acquire a new skill. New skills increase your opportunities for work and may also upgrade your hourly rate.

Timesheets

Every THC has its own timesheets and payment schedule. The timesheet will ask for your name, social security number, client company, job classification, and hours worked. The THC may require you to phone in your hours the day before payday. This gives the accounting department time to issue checks. Have your supervisor sign your timesheet on due day, and either bring it over to the THC to collect your check or fax it with a note asking them to mail your check to you. Some THCs even offer direct deposit. If you do not have any blank timesheets, ask the THC if you can present a letter on client stationary signed by the supervisor. Remember to deduct the appropriate number of hours for lunch. If you've worked through lunch hour, you might have to spread the hours over the course of the day or week as some cities do not permit employees to work eight hours straight without a break. If you have any questions on filling out timesheets, call your counselor.

Dress Like the Others

If you're working in a corporate environment, dress professionally on the first day (as described in Chapter 15), unless told otherwise. There will be those times you'll find yourself completely overdressed, but that's better than the reverse situation. Jackets can always be taken off, and you can show up the next day with a more informal look. If you feel you're overdressed, ask your supervisor if you can opt for a more casual approach. It's not professional to dress down on purpose "just because you're a Temp." I've met too many Temps decked out completely in black, in casual slacks, mis-matched socks, wearing six earrings in one or more ears, and who wore the same shirt for days on end. In short, if you want to be respected for being the professional contingency worker you are, look the part.

Some Don't's

I'm almost embarrassed by all the "Should's" and "Do's" I've stated in this book. Let's conclude this chapter by presenting a brief check-list of some important **Don't's**. These are common sense items, which can cost you an assignment or ostracize you from a THC Temp pool altogether.

- Don't get too chummy with your counselor, fellow Temps, or full-time employees met at the job site.
- Don't gossip with or about fellow Temps, employees, or counselors.
- Don't make your political, social, or religious views the talk of the office.
- Don't try to resolve conflicts directly with the client.
- Don't discuss salary issues with anyone at the client company.
- Don't call the client if you're going to be late or if you're ill. Notify the THC. In the event of accident, illness, or death in the family, you must notify or have someone notify the THC posthaste so they can secure a replacement.
- Don't help yourself to any equipment or supplies at the job site.
- Don't accept any assignments you do not feel comfortable with.
- Don't get too settled in. This means no personal files on the computers, no slippers, photos of the kids on the desk, plants, pets, children, personal calls (made or received), mail, and so forth.

- NEVER, approach the client about in-house work until you have completed your assignment. This is a fundamental taboo. Temps frequently cannot resist the temptation to "strike a deal" with clients. They have signed a contract with the THC promising not to hire any Temp as an in-house or full-time employee without paying a substantial fee. Trying to work around this arrangement puts the client at legal and financial risk, and no matter how good a worker you are, the client will not jeopardize its reputation for you. Your attempt to do so imparts to the client that: (1) you have no respect for their legal position, (2) you are interested only in securing higher pay, and (3) the very fact that you will work "twice as hard" indicates you are not giving them your best effort.

  In short, no matter how good and original this idea seems to you, forget it. It's been tried a million times before. If, however, you are a college student working during the summer, you can inquire if the client can hire you in-house during intercession or other school breaks, provided they occur at least three months after your assignment ends. If the client wants to hire you as a full-time employee, have them initiate the process directly with the THC. Further, if the client should try to "steal" you from the THC by offering to "split the difference," notify your counselor at once. You might lose that particular assignment, but the counselor will undoubtedly remember your honesty and integrity.

- Finally, NEVER, EVER, EVER engage in illegal activities. Should there be narcotics at the workplace, run the other way. If you suspect substance abuse at the job site, call your counselor immediately. If there are people around, go to a pay phone outside. Likewise, don't participate in sports pools, be sure to honor the company's position on smoking, and avoid alcohol during working hours.

CHAPTER TWENTY

Interpersonal Relationships

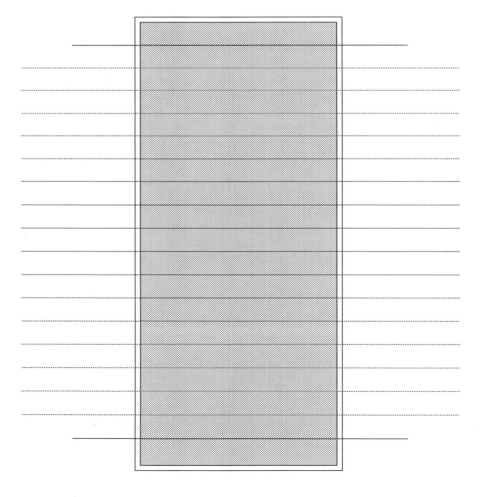

I make no pretense to being an expert in psychology or interpersonal relations. But after dealing with dozens of different types in the work environment, I've come to realize that although there's a plethora of personalities out there, one finds many common denominators.

Interpersonal Relations

As a Temp, the onus is on you to work with different and sometimes difficult people. This holds true not only for office support personnel and laborers, but for technical and professional persons as well. A chemist friend of mine was admonished no less than seven times on his first day at a new Temp assignment by a lab assistant that "He didn't do it like that." What did my friend do differently from the boss? He didn't: (1) remove jars from the refrigerator like he did; (2) light a match the same way; (3) draw blood using the same technique; (4) take tissue samples his way; (5) prepare slides in exactly the same manner; and two other procedures that escape me at the moment. By 5:00 my friend was completely aggravated. He considered calling his consulting firm and requesting another assignment. Instead, he took a gamble in dealing directly with the supervisor. He said, "You know what, why don't we just go downstairs to Biotechnology and have them clone you so you can have someone who does everything exactly the way you do." The other scientist's reaction? He just laughed and said, "C'mon, let's go get something to eat." My friend was able to get through to the fellow because they were on a par professionally. Most of us, however, are obliged to contact our counselors should any problems arise.

To settle any conflicts, you need a solid foundation. First, establish a good relationship with your THC. They're counting on you to be professional and diplomatic. It is simply not productive to tell off a difficult manager. If you wind up with an abusive or overly demanding boss, ask your counselor for advice. Sometimes the counselor will remind you you're there only for a day or two and ask you to acquiesce to the boss as a favor. This particular challenge should be thought of as an act of good faith, evidence that the counselor has confidence in you to overcome obstacles. Counselors will intervene if there is a history of problems with a particular client supervisor or other employees. Truly abusive situations do demand intervention and the THC will act accordingly.

There are a few important points to consider. First of all, as a Temp, you have been requisitioned, or ordered, much like a new typewriter or lunch. The client is not interested that you're Lewis, or Cheryl, or Paula, or Bob, or Keith, or Lance, or Natasha, or Mimi, or Shira. It is irrelevant that you are an unemployed lawyer, social worker, graduate student, actor, widow, mother, son, daughter, or that you've been a priest, baseball hero, or Fulbright scholar.

Some clients will consider you just a body needed to perform a particular function. Others will be cordial, helpful, and appreciative. Temps must be thick-skinned, and you simply cannot arrive at a new Temp assignment with a delicate ego. Once you understand the social contract, half the battle is won.

How can you empower yourself to make a good impression on people at the job site? The fundamental ingredient in my recipe for cooking up a successful Temp is to remember that you **represent and work for** the THC. Remember how up-beat and cheery your counselor seems all the time? Learn from that. From your very first assignment, you must give the impression you are completely calm. There are no first-day jitters, at least none that anyone can detect. Give the impression you are a seasoned professional, even if this is your very first assignment.

The second ingredient is to leave your personal agenda at home. Say very little about yourself. Volunteer nothing. Let your competence and congeniality speak for you. I've worked at some assignments for three or four weeks before anyone asked me if I lived in the area. No one has to know if you are married or what your hobbies are. People are naturally curious about strangers, and by keeping your personal life a mystery, at least some people will try hard to be friendly.

Give it time. Let THEM discover who you are!

Let's enumerate some of the salient points about interpersonal interactions on the job:

- Be cordial and respectful to others.
- Be relaxed from the moment you walk in.
- Be confident in your abilities.
- Disclose little about yourself.
- Leave your personal agenda at home.
- Don't take things as personal assaults; think of yourself as an actor playing the part of a contingent worker whom the client has requisitioned.
- Ask questions if you need help, but always be tactful and polite.
- If things get out of hand, call your THC and ask your counselor to intervene.

Managers

There are many kinds of managers out there. Within a short time, you'll come across many of them!

A manager, or supervisor, is the person at the job site to whom you report. The manager may assign the tasks to the employees, and he or she is often the person who reviews the work. Managers may be senior clerks, executive secretaries, plant foremen, lawyers, accountants, physicians, vice presidents, or chief executive officers.

Three factors come into play in your relationship with managers. First, there's the issue of your job assignment. If you are hired to work on an assembly line, chances are you will have no interaction with the executives. The foreman or plant manager is there to make sure everyone knows what is expected of him/her and that production levels are met. In a word processing pool, especially in legal environments, the supervisor manages work-flow and might also proofread your work. Secretarial positions are structured so that you work closely with the boss.

The second issue concerns the rank of your boss. For example, a senior clerk is down in the field working with you, whereas a vice president is quite removed from the acts of typing memos, sending faxes, and assembling better mousetraps. Finally, there is the personality of the individual in question, and it's your task to acclimatize quickly.

A good manager will recognize your abilities. More often than not, I have been treated with respect at the work place. But I have also worked with people who were difficult. Some managers may not have a clue as to how to interact with people, pay a compliment, or impart constructive criticism. They may not be good at communicating their ideas and make no effort to conceal the fact that their regular secretary or assistant is the best in the world. As a professional, you should never be offended personally.

Keep in mind that some managers are yellers. Yellers are insecure and should be humored. I recently worked for one who asked me to "send over" a letter that had come to him by mistake via fax to a manager in a different building. As he had not made it clear if he meant to send it through interoffice mail or fax, I asked, "Do you want me to fax this?" His temper flared. He shouted for all to hear, "That's what I thought I said," to which I replied firmly, "I'm sorry, but had I heard what you said I wouldn't have asked you. I'll do it right now." As a professional, keep in mind that diplomacy is always the better part of valor.

Managers can sometimes push you to your limit and then some. This kind of behavior is usually due more to thoughtlessness than malice. A

Temp can't possibly come in cold knowing the personalities and responsibilities of the persons he or she is working for. Further, the person for whom the Temp is substituting, assuming there is such a person, will forever be a mystery. When difficulties arise, keep in mind:

1. The person(s) you are replacing or substituting for is perceived to be unparalleled at his or her job and you are simply no match. The manager might resent having to settle for someone less than perfect.

2. The manager hasn't thought to show you where things are and help you perform certain tasks that the regular full-time employees normally fulfill without any hesitation.

3. The manager doesn't understand that you have no vested interest in the company and will not work additional hours without compensation.

Some managers are themselves in no-win situations and are compelled by their superiors to make every effort to conserve paper clips, rubber bands, and so forth. They are often forced to work long hours and meet quotas. Chances are they will be appreciative of your efforts, even if they don't impart this to you. But there are those who will never praise your work. You give them something, they say "It's okay, I suppose." And that worried look on their face tells you they're scared to death of the person above them. Again, don't take them personally.

Sometimes you'll be lucky enough to come across a Wonder Woman or Superman clone. These top-notch managers take their jobs very seriously but still have time for human interactions. They demand high standards but at the same time make the people around them feel good about themselves. It is always a pleasure to work for these people, and there is plenty one can learn from them.

Most managers are delighted to have someone competent working for them. They will treat you like gold, praise your work, remind you to help yourself to coffee, and request you in the future whenever they need a Temp.

Co-Workers

Co-workers are also a diverse group. Some will be resentful that a mere Temp has been brought in to work with them. Sometimes you can quickly identify why they act stand-offish. You are, after all, sitting in the seat of a co-worker of theirs. You might be "burdening" them by asking for the key to the restroom twice a day. Behavior like this is rare and most full-timers will be accommodating. Depending upon the nature and structure of the work-place, and the logistics of desks and seating, your proximity and association with other people can vary from nil to eight hours straight of intimate collaboration.

Sometime down the road you might come across a disgruntled full-time employee or two who'll want to tell you their whole life story. If you have a non-stop talker who complains unremittingly about other employees, how busy he/she is, or a sister-in-law's poor taste in clothing, confront this person in a nice but firm manner. Apologize for your inability to digest their entire life history while you're trying to de-bug a computer program or decipher a manager's poor handwriting. Tell them, "Oh, gee, I'm so sorry to hear that, but I've really got to concentrate on this or they'll have my hide." If the one-way conversation doesn't let up, speak with a manager about possibly moving your work station. You may also find motherly and paternal types who'll feel sorry you're "just a Temp," those who are dying to leave their jobs and see you as a window through which they can "break into Temping," and others who'll display a genuine interest in your personal well-being and/or creative endeavors.

It's not a good idea to attempt to become "one of the guys/girls," because, to put it bluntly, you're not. You are there for a limited period of time whereas these people have been and will continue to remain there considerably longer. While you need only make a few phone calls and presto, you're at a new assignment, the job site is for them a second home. They would be utterly foolish to jeopardize their bread and butter by spending lots of time socializing with "the Temp" during work hours. Interestingly, however, any resentment on their part is sometimes symptomatic of the indignation that they will not have enough time to get to know **everything** about you.

Consultants and in-house Temp experience completely different relationships with co-workers. Freelancers and consultants generally enjoy underlying respect because they are hired to perform specific tasks that require someone with skills not readily available among the full-time employees. In-house Temps are essentially spurious employees in that they look and act like full-time employees, are accountable to the company, are on the company's payroll, and work directly with full-time employees but do not qualify for company benefits.

One question that pops up incessantly on assignments is "What do you really do?"[1] I myself ask it of fellow Temps, but in jest. Co-workers at the job site sometimes hope you'll admit to being that young actor they once saw on a "Pizza Hut" commercial.

You can avoid answering the question by saying you've worked for Such & Such Temporary Help Company for the past six months. Period. This kind of answer intimates you're not really interested in saying you're Temping while trying to master origami or your husband's balloon business busted and you've got to work to make the mortgage payments. If you want to share why you are Temping do so, but succinctly. Above all, don't impart any negative feelings. Remember, you're a professional. Making this your mantra will avert potential conflicts.

Finally, **do not** intimate to co-workers that you would like to become a full-time employee at the company. This is something to discuss with managers or human resources. Check the internal job-postings at the client company. If anything interests you, discuss the possibilities with your supervisor, and make sure your counselor is notified immediately if the client company wishes to hire you directly.

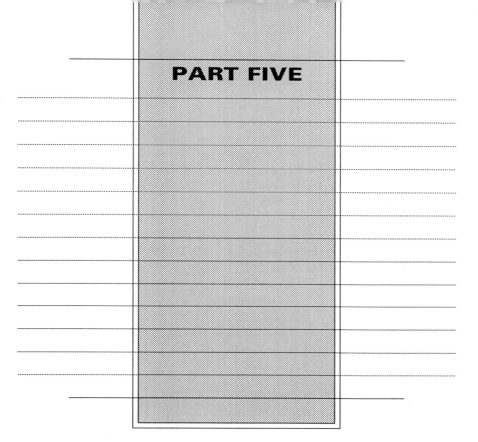

PART FIVE

Other Issues

CHAPTER TWENTY-ONE

Not Getting Work?

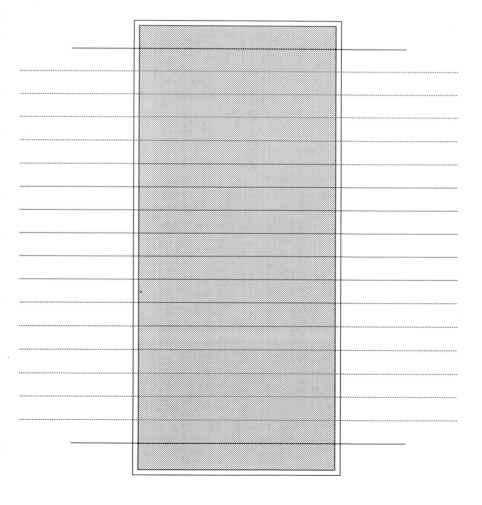

I t's one of the most frustrating things in the world. You're all dressed up with no place to go. You've gotten up at 7:00 A.M., showered, dressed, eaten a light breakfast, and are ready to leave for work. The day's wages are pretty much indispensable, and you need to feel useful and productive. You called your THCs yesterday afternoon and were told they'd call you in the morning. They haven't. Perhaps it's too early. You wait a few more minutes then call them. Your counselor answers the phone. It's only 8:15 A.M., but already the THC staff is hard at work.

The Initial Jolt

"Sorry, nothing's come in yet. Call me in a half-hour." You say fine, talk to you later, and hang up. Now what to do? Get the kids off to school? Turn on *Good Morning America*? Trace the development of spoken Bulgarian?

Time passes. You call again. The counselor assures you of a call-back. If you haven't been assigned by ten o'clock, you might get a call from a counselor who'll say something like, "I know you live in Cedar Rapids, but if you can be in Des Moines in fifteen minutes, I've got a one-day for you," or you'll call again and hear, "Nothing's come in yet, but I'm working on it. Gimme a call back at 3:30."

So, it's either back to bed, tackling the day's chores, or off to the library. Sometimes you'll experience a feeling of relief, but other times you will suffer that pang in your stomach that signifies a mixture of panic and frustration. You know you did everything correctly and played by the rules, but you're still going to have a down-day.

What Went Wrong?

"What went wrong?" That's the underlying question. You really don't know if somehow you are responsible for not getting work on any given day. Each case is individual, and although there's a myriad of possibilities, we can reduce these to three categories:

1. Market factors;
2. The THC's business is soft; or, hard to believe;
3. You are doing something wrong or are perceived to be doing something wrong.

You can still do a few things to improve your chances of getting work. You have plenty of opportunities to market yourself by using your free day to register with additional THCs. You can put together a new résumé and perhaps work on your skills at home, the library, or a local job training center. If you suspect you're the culprit, cut your hair, polish your shoes, refrain from dressing completely in black, quit smoking, learn to smile, or do **whatever** it takes to clear up any negative images client or THC might have of you and present yourself as a winner. Let's look at these areas in general terms.

Market Factors

The economic slump of the late 1980s was first felt in the Temping industry in the aftermath of the stock market crises of October 26, 1987, "Black Monday." The acknowledgment of America as a post-Industrialization power and the economic uncertainties of the prospect of war in the Persian Gulf further aggravated the situation, forcing many companies to restructure. Because Temps are used mainly for work overloads and special projects, this translated into fewer Temp jobs. Whereas in the past, lay-offs were counterbalanced with hiring Temps, and retirees were replaced with trainees, companies nowadays turn to internal transfers, cross-training, overtime, or just plain overworking their employees. Adding to the diminishing Temp requisitions is the marked increase in qualified applicants. A cross-section of American society can now be found in any THC reception area. More students are desperately seeking summer employment and more recent college graduates are willing to spend their days as file clerks just to get their feet in the door. Also, a greater number of retirees need to work to make ends meet, and a profusion of job-hungry, highly skilled and not-so-highly-skilled workers and displaced military personnel abounds.

Some seasons are worse than others. Temporary summer replacements are still needed, especially for administrative and executive assistants. Yet this increase in demand is offset by the large number of college students seeking summer employment. Further, many people see fit to resign full-time positions in June in order to free up their summers. Temping permits them to work sporadically so they have plenty of time to go to the beach. Certain industries, such as banking, law, and international exporting experience summer lulls. In short, there is little you can do to rectify economic and political impact. But you can increase your chances of securing work by:

- Registering with additional THCs to increase prospects.
- Aggressively lobbying your favorite THCs. You can just "drop by on your way to the mall" or send a thank-you note to your counselors saying something like "I know it's been slow, but I just wanted to say thanks for really pushing for me." Whether the counselor has tried to place you or not is a moot point; it makes them feel good, serves as a reminder you're out there, and shows some degree of empathy that their commissions are down as well.
- Contacting in-house Temp services, particularly those companies where you've worked before. For companies that don't have an in-house service, try calling some of your former supervisors or co-workers to see if they could entice human resources into offering you freelance work or asking for you when they call your THC.
- Using your down-time creatively. Ask your counselors if the THC can provide training to help you increase your skills set and subsequent marketability. Basic bookkeeping, computers, LAN administration, word processing, and editing and proofreading are viable options. Everyone will benefit from this because the more you earn, the greater the THC's revenues and the counselor's commissions. Maybe a business course at a community college or adult-education center is in order. Don't forget to check the career books section of your local library for additional information (See Appendix B for suggestions).
- Brainstorm with a friend. Two heads are better than one, and bouncing ideas off each other can open up a world of opportunities.

THC Considerations

Let's face it, some THCs work harder than others. And some counselors are more talented than their colleagues. In general, counselors rally to find work for their Temps. Well-established THCs often enjoy long-standing and exclusive relationships with various clients. The clients know they can count on the THC to fill their orders with a qualified Temp immediately. Local clients frequently arrange to train selected members of a THC's Temp pool to work for them on long-term assignments. Everybody benefits from these symbiotic relationships. The clients get discounted pricing, the THCs enjoy steady customers and are spared training expenses, and the Temps get some sense of job security.

Younger and smaller THCs, however, must aggressively seek new business. If their marketing people are anything short of top-notch you may not get steady work. Often, marketing people will accept or place, depending upon context, a lower bid to secure and maintain a client.

The THC might charge fifty cents or a dollar an hour below scale to win over a new client. This means you will be asked to accept a lower rate as well. In a favorable economic climate, it is a difficult judgment call. Hurt pride aside, can you afford to work for $9 an hour instead of your normal rate of $11? Why does the newspaper advertisement specify $18 an hour for WordPerfect™ secretaries when they in fact are only offering $15? False advertising? Was it just a ploy to recruit new Temps? Regardless of the rationale, it's not worth the time, energy, or money to enact a class action suit.

Once I had a two-week assignment at the building planning division of a teaching hospital for $1.50 an hour below my regular rate. I was not thrilled with this arrangement because, coincidentally, I had just priced treatment at that hospital and found it prohibitive. I jokingly told my counselor she should find me someone to fix my uninsured jaw for ten bucks an hour. She asked me to "do her a favor" and accept it, and, as I did not have another prospect, I agreed and promised to give it my best shot. It turned out that the group members with whom I worked comprised the nicest people I had ever encountered on a Temp assignment. The environment thus compensated for the lower pay scale. I was able to bargain up my fee a little when I returned to the hospital for other assignments.

Is it the THC, the economy, or both? I returned to one THC after an eight-month hiatus and found that two counselors had been let go. The work area had been restructured, and people were no longer being paid for stand-by. Interviews were now by appointment only, and the coffee machine had been moved from the reception area to the counselor section. The marketing people looked frazzled, and one of the counselors I have known for several years had lost weight and had noticeable bags under his eyes. Another THC I returned to after two years had moved into a cramped suite it shared with a three-person real estate company, a self-employed accountant, and a lawyer who negotiated wills and personal bankruptcies. Like most people, counselors are working harder for less compensation.

Is It Me?

Before you panic, ask yourself these questions: (For those who have worked for a THC before)—Did I do well on my last assignment(s)?, Could anyone have given me an unflattering review?, Was I pleasant, punctual, presentable, proficient, and professional?, and Did I ever give my THC cause for concern (e.g., turn down more than one assignment in the past month, leave an assignment before completion, etc.)?

And (For those who only recently registered with a THC)—Are my skills up to par? Did my interview go well? Was I available immediately and for an indefinite period? Did I come off professional, gracious, and confident? Did I leave my dental appointment, sick dog, term paper, or whatever else personal agenda at home?

Temp applicants are a dime a dozen. Good Temps are another matter. Giving reason to doubt your abilities seriously imperils your chances for getting work. Personal agendas, conflicts, problems, concerns, and lifestyles need to be put on hold during work hours, Concentrate on building your skill sets and winning approval. If you've done your homework on relating to people, increased and sharpened your skills, made an agreeable impression on clients, represented your THC like a pro, and still experience many down-days, register with additional THCs. Read your local newspaper and watch the nightly news to get a sense of economic indicators as well. An economic slump means more people out of work, more people in the Temp pool, and fewer jobs to go around. But if you're personable and competent, you should do fine.

CHAPTER TWENTY-TWO

Attitudes and Expectations

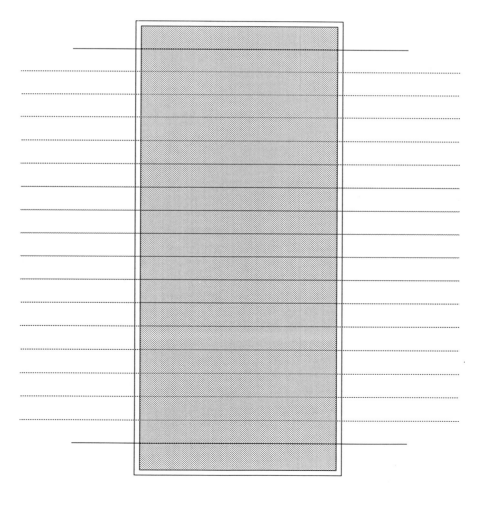

Temps in big cities are sometimes leery of being taken advantage of by their counselors and client bosses. Occasionally their apprehensions are justified.

What to Expect

Once in a while counselors may try to talk you into accepting or remaining at an assignment you would prefer not to. Make an effort to go along with the counselor wishes, whenever possible. They know the market and they know what they're doing. Complying might bring you additional assignments or better pay. Of course, if you really can't stand the job or the people you should insist they send in a replacement. If the counselor becomes angry and does not offer you work after that, break off your association with that THC and register with another.

When filling in for a secretary or administrative assistant the manager in question might not concede you are not that person. Many times I've heard something to the effect, "When you go down, would you bring me back a tuna on toast and a Diet Pepsi?" This is right up there with "Could you wash my coffee cup?" and "I need you to get my wife a birthday card." I sometimes oblige the sandwich request if, at that moment I'm going out for lunch or if I can bill the client for the extra time spent in line at the food counter. If I have to order in lunch and I know for sure the company is going to pick up the tab, I occasionally ask if I can order something myself, especially if I'm going to be working through lunch or will be putting in overtime.

I don't mind taking my turn at making the coffee as long as I can have my share. However, I am not a technician, so repairing photocopy machines, other than removing a sheet of paper jammed in a machine I'm using, is out of the question. An office support Temp should not be expected to clean windows, water plants, or shine shoes, unless specifically requested to do so by the counselor **before** agreeing to take the assignment.

Getting to work is sometimes a problem. Your THC should use discretion in assigning you to a location. If you live in a "car town," common sense should preclude a counselor from assigning you to a location more than forty miles from home. Only a foolish counselor would send someone a great distance, unless the THC will compensate you for the commute.

Client managers may forget you're a human being, not SuperTemp flying through the sky at their beck and call. We, too, are subject to traffic jams, stalled trains, and the nightmare of urban commuting. I had a long-term assignment for which I had to take a bus to the subway (twenty-five minutes), ride the train for a half hour, change for another train (another fifteen minutes), then walk briskly for another ten minutes. Because of the extensive track repair work that summer, the trip was sometimes stretched to two hours and I was invariably late, even when I left my apartment early. Several full-time personnel were also consistently late, but it seemed I was the only one admonished. I eventually discussed the issue with my counselor, who honored my request to be re-assigned to a better location.

If you find yourself stuck in bumper-to-bumper traffic, pull off the highway and get to a phone as soon as possible. Call the THC, not the client. If you're trapped in a subway car going nowhere quickly, there's little you can do except to call once you've gotten to the appropriate station; of course, if you're bumped off a train call your counselor immediately.

A Caustic Caveat

There are still people out there who mistrust Temps and propagate the old myths and half-truths. Others will believe them. Despite all the hard-core data to the contrary, we still come across commentaries such as this one, entitled "Too Many Temps":

> "A troubling trend in the workplace could thwart the Clinton Administration's plans to help American employees become more productive and the businesses they work for more competitive.
>
> "Personnel managers have several names for this trend: contingency work, just-in-time employment and employee leasing. An older term for it is temporary employment.
>
> "Today, almost 20 million American working men and women, rather than being gainfully employed, hold "contingency" jobs, many of them part-time. These jobs offer neither security nor benefits to employees, and to employers, neither the productivity levels of their permanent employees nor the chance for long-term growth.

"Personnel managers' promises of short-term cost savings for their clients already ring hollow. Numerous studies have shown that temporary employees are significantly less productive than permanent employees and that workers become demoralized when they see a low ceiling on their potential for long-term employment. . . ."[1]

The commentator was Al Bilik, President of the Public Employment Department of the AFL–CIO. The Federal government has in fact utilized the growing number of Temp jobs as an indicator of overall job-growth, the result being a spurious economic recovery, but the use of Temps does not jeopardize industry in general. Indeed, those workers who are disheartened by the lack of a Temp-to-Permanent guarantee have misinterpreted the temporary employee's social contract. Temps enjoy flexibility, the opportunity to see different work environments, disinterest from corporate politics, and responsibility for securing their own insurance plans, often with some contribution from their THCs. Old attitudes die hard making it even more essential for Temps to discredit them through honest and dependable work.

In today's market, any criticizing attitudes towards Temps are ironic. Companies need contingency workers to fulfill certain tasks, yet at the same time they're uneasy about anyone who's available to do so. Fortunately, most employers have developed a sensitized environment and concede there are many good people out there with excellent abilities. In dealing with insecure or overly aggressive people, be especially diplomatic and remember that placement counselors are aware that some managers and full-time employees are difficult.

Money Matters

Conflict resolution is best left to your THC. If you are sent out as a clerk/typist and find yourself having to operate a complicated memory typewriter or mainframe terminal all day, an error in job classification has been made, most likely by the client. If the clerk/typist duties involve typing numbers in charts and columns for hours on end, you in fact are doing statistical typing, which involves a premium. If you are hired as a word processing secretary and upon arrival are sent to the word processing pool of a legal department and must use a dictaphone, you again have been misclassified. If you believe the job classification is different from the one you agreed to in the first place, call your THC at the earliest opportunity. If you are a freelancer, ask to speak with the human resources administrator who contracted your terms.

Communication problems abound, and companies inexperienced in working with Temps still have a lot to learn. For instance, I accepted a one-day spot at a small production firm to type advertising copy. When I arrived, I found a very buoyant team and a full in-box. I set out to type the copy and at 1:00 P.M. asked if I could go for lunch. The office manager inquired how the work was progressing, and I told her that the in-box materials were now in the out-box and I would be ready for a refill when I returned in a half hour. She commented on how quickly I was able to finish the job and asked for my timesheet. Stunned, I asked why. She replied, "That's all there is." I reminded her that the THC had a four-hour minimum assignment policy, whether the Temp is actually needed for that amount of time or not, and that I was told the assignment would last the entire day.

Without uttering a word, she lifted the receiver to her ear and dialed the THC. She spoke to my counselor and accused me of unprofessional behavior. She hung up and said, "Three hours, period." I asked to use the phone and dialed my counselor for instructions. The counselor said I should let her sign for the three hours but the THC would make good on the additional hour. I was annoyed that my counselor sent me to an assignment without verifying the minimum number of hours and did not offer to compensate me for the entire day. That was the last time I worked for that particular service.

CHAPTER TWENTY-THREE

Common Complaints

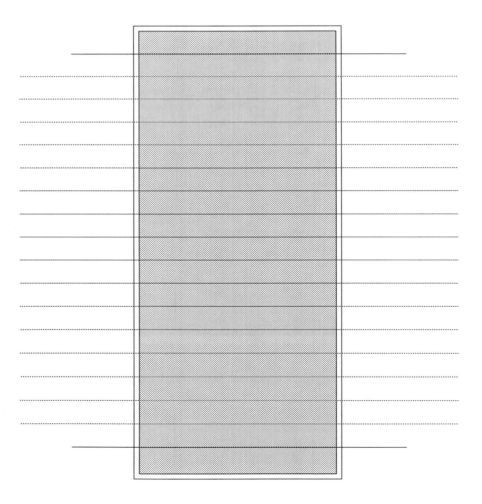

Counselors always try to compromise, and you need to keep an opened mind. In the job situation described in Chapter 22, the client regarded the Temp as a disposable object to have around for a couple of hours to service them before he or she marches blithely on to the next appointment. This "that's-all-we-need-you-for" mid-day termination is one of the more ignoble and frustrating hardships we occasionally endure. If the counselor does not support you in your grievance, you are out of luck.

Miscommunication

The client showed poor judgment in its use of a Temp. They violated their contract with the THC and did not utilize me for other work that could have been done. At another assignment, a manager told me after lunch, "Just finish entering this data in the system, and then I've got a surprise for you." The "surprise" was that I got to go home early, without pay, though she "gave me" an extra half-hour on the timesheet. I believe she honestly thought she was doing something nice and could not understand why I didn't jump up and down shouting "hurray." It never crossed her mind that her half-hour "gift" still put me $42 behind budget. "Thanks, that's-all-we-need-you-for" signifies the client's thoughtlessness toward best utilizing a qualified helper as well as a disregard for contractual obligations.

Temps have other complaints as well. The disposable person situation is symptomatic of a circumstance many call "Second Class Citizenship." Of the hundreds of Temps I've spoken with about "Second Class Citizenship," the answer is always the same: the lack of benefits. Some technical and professional Temps, nurses in particular, find they have little outlet for making decisions. The circumstances are different for consultants specially hired to design systems. Career Temps often are not as seriously affected by all this because they Temp only to have steady income while pursuing their other agendas.

There are other grounds for some Temps to sometimes feel like "Second Class Citizens." Freelancers periodically run into trouble getting paid because some companies are slow in issuing checks. Temps working through THCs or on an in-house basis, however, are paid regularly without any difficulties.

Consultants and freelancers in higher wage brackets should have the client sign contracts that lock the project into a minimum time vector or at least guarantee a minimum fee. Freelancers working in general office support, light industrial, or technical areas usually have to rely on verbal agreements but still enjoy some leeway in negotiating terms and conditions. Contracts prevent the client from dismissing them for no apparent reason. In-house Temps are sometimes at a disadvantage because they have neither contract nor third-party to back them up. Chances are, however, if the client has agreed to hire you as an in-house Temp, they plan to keep you around for a while.

Additional Temp Criticisms

Company Holidays

My friend Estelle is a gem. Fifty-eight years old, divorced longer than married, and the mother of six adult children, Estelle has been Temping for four years. Estelle refers to company holidays as "The Killer-Days." After working for three years as a Permanent Temp clerk at a Fortune 100 company, she bemoans the fact that her boss has never yielded even one hour's extra pay, despite her never being absent. Last December she divulged to me,

> "Here it is, Christmas time, and they're having parties twice a week for a month. So they close early on Friday one week, then the next week's the night before Christmas Eve, so we're out at 3:00. Then it's Christmas Eve, and we're out at 1:00, then it's Christmas Day and the Day after Christmas. At least last year Christmas was on a Sunday, so I didn't get gypped out of two days. It just infuriates me that I'm out almost three hundred bucks while they're all getting wasted on 'holiday cheer!'"

Estelle calculated that legal and company holidays (President's Day, Memorial Day, Independence Day, Labor Day, Columbus Day, Thanksgiving, Christmas Eve and Day, and New Year's Eve and Day, among others) result in $600 to $700 a year in lost income. She feels that having Temped in-house for so long warrants at least some sort of compensation for company holidays or at the very least, early-closings. But in 1989 the company did away with all such compensation for in-house Temps, and Estelle and a hundred or so others had no recourse. The client has yet to learn that permitting someone to take a one-week vacation with pay, or, at the very least, compensate the few dollars they lose when it closes early for holidays, makes the Temp feel better about the employer and about themselves.

This small, inexpensive courtesy could assuage much of the "Second Class Citizen" feeling. Companies need to realize that the resulting goodwill makes for a happier and better worker, and in the end all parties benefit. Perhaps compensation for company half-days can be extended to Temps who work a specified number of hours. Human resources executives should carefully weigh the cost factor against the human rewards.

Sick Days

Temps are not paid for time off due to illness. If you are a THC Temp and cannot make it to the job site because you're sick, call your counselor as soon as the THC opens so he or she can line up a replacement.

Be prudent in asking for sick time while engaged in an assignment. In other words, **don't** say you're sick if you're not. Most THCs understand that you are human and things happen, and they will make every effort to secure a replacement for you and arrange for you to return to the job site when you are able to, provided the assignment continues beyond that time.

I only once experienced a problem with a THC regarding a sick day. I suffered a debilitating tension headache from working a data entry job in front of an old IBM "green screens." I called the THC to say I couldn't go in, but when the counselor insisted I finish the assignment I became angry and told her that it was because of the monitor that I was sick in the first place! I lost that position and waited nearly a month before they called me again.

Perhaps the counselor didn't handle the situation diplomatically, but neither did I. I should not have made accusations. Rather, I should have just said that I was too sick and left it at that. If you become ill on the job, notify your counselor immediately. No one will expect you to sit there if you are too uncomfortable to work. A sympathetic client might even arrange transportation home for you.

Large corporations sometimes maintain their own medical departments which provide free primary medical attention to employees in emergency situations and make referrals for more comprehensive care. Such services are rarely available to Temps. Companies justify this on the grounds that their professional liability coverage does not extend to treating non-employees. In some instances, it may be more a case of denying a perk to Temps in an effort to keep down operating expenses.

If you are in need of medical attention while on the job, either call or have someone else call your counselor.

Company Events

I recently received an anonymous E-mail message from a 29-year-old male technical Temp relating the following story:

> "I've been Temping at an engineering firm for four months now. I do all the work of an independent consultant, but I'm still classified as a Temp because I work for Temp agency rather than a consulting firm. My paycheck also reminds me that I'm not a real consultant. I manage a team of four, two of them Temps, two of them regular employees. Anyway, the company was having its summer picnic and I signed up to go, and three days later someone from human resources calls me up and says in a real snotty voice, 'J____, you can't go to the picnic. You're only a Temp and you gotta be here for six months.' Boy, I was angry. I can't believe it . . . I'm managing people here and I can't get a lousy hot dog or play volley ball with them."

I understand this man's frustration. The event seemed like fun, with plenty of fresh air, food, and outdoor activities. Although he's fulfilling the role of a team player, the company bureaucracy prevented him from being treated as one. Yet some company events can be irritating, and as a Temp you don't have to be concerned with them. Christmas parties and the like are the obligation of the full-timers. You can spend special events with the people of your choice and not have to worry about "being seen." As for company sponsored can-food collections, United Way presentations, and blood drives, make your donations of time, money, clothing, and bodily fluids on your own time, outside the work environment.

Inaccurate Job Descriptions

Inaccurate job descriptions can lead to salary misclassification. In the event of a misunderstanding in duties, notify your counselor at once. Misunderstandings include using a software package other than that specified by the counselor, finding yourself doing statistical rather than text typing, graphics rather than word processing, skilled labor rather than unskilled, and so forth.

Clients who misinform wind up frustrating all parties concerned. Once, however, I was on the "giving end" instead of receiving end. When my status at one company changed from THC Temp to in-house Temp, I took an up front two-week vacation. The boss requisitioned a Temp to fill in for me. The Temp arrived the day before I left, giving us a day to work together so I could show her the ropes. My boss had to send the requisition to Human Resources but could not reveal to them that he had installed some of his personal software on a company computer. The Temp showed up knowing only DOS programs and was stymied by the Windows environment and the mouse. All through my vacation I called the office twice a day (collect, of course) and talked her through different formatting problems until she eventually caught on. My heart went out to her every time she asked me why they didn't tell her about the Windows environment, but I just couldn't reveal that the programs did not have company sanction. On other occasions, managers themselves are not fully aware of software packages or procedures when they place the order, so misinformation is passed on to the THC.

Diplomat-*cum*-Therapist

At times you might find yourself in the unlucky predicament of acting as a therapist to a crabby boss. This situation arises when a manager is not sure of your capabilities or what exactly to expect of you. They might not be effective communicators or they lack interpersonal skills. Perhaps they don't trust you because they don't know "where you're coming from."

To avoid problems, always ask for a coordinated work flow. Distance yourself from the environment's history, hierarchy, and politics, and be upbeat while at the same time maintaining au aura of calm professionalism. Dump any negative feelings when you leave for the day, and remember that you're earning a decent wage and have no ties to any one company.

Temp Agreements

Some large companies have recently begun to ask contingency workers to sign "Temp Agreements." These documents are legal instruments in which the Temp or consultant agrees to sundry conditions, such as not to steal company secrets. They may be asked to transfer their rights to any materials they might have written for the company, follow the company codes relating to dress, smoking, ethics, and so on. Companies might also stipulate that in-house Temps waive their rights to sue for health insurance contributions.

However, these provisions can conflict with state regulations and may be contested in court. If you accept a long-term in-house contingency position and are asked to sign a "Temp agreement," photocopy the instrument in question and notify your local labor department that same day.

Problem Situations

Problems arise when there's a misunderstanding on the part of the client, THC, or the Temp. You can avoid hassles by assuming a "teflon personality" and let all negative things bounce off you.

I've had two especially difficult bosses, both of whom demonstrated low self-esteem, which made their interactions with others difficult. One was the administrative assistant of an accounting firm who told me up front I was the third Temp that week. She said she expected someone to get the work done without any complaints or "back talk" and that she was in the process of suing the company for personal injury compensation and punitive damages.

Later that morning we had trouble with the printers. Realizing that the printer had not been set correctly that morning and we needed only to flip a switch to fix it, I suggested we both exit the program, return to the main menu, reconfigure the printer switch, then try to print again. But instead, she called technical support for a computer technician. I said, "Could I just re-configure the —" to which she snapped, "No, you don't just do nothing—you're only a Temp." A technician eventually arrived, flipped the switch, and we were back in business.

Clearly, her poor self-image, coupled with her pending lawsuit against the company, precluded any sort of rational thought. To meet this challenge, I made an extra effort to only nod in approval with whatever she said. I made sure to answer the phones by the second ring, do my work quickly, and always appear busy.

At the other assignment I served as an interim secretary at a realty firm. The vice president was hardworking and dedicated, putting in 10-hour days. However, the self-esteem factor again came into play, and I was greeted with a simple, "This is your desk. Hold my calls and I'll be out in a half hour to talk to you." During the day the phones rang constantly. I had endless photocopies to make, files to maintain, and heavy word processing.

The filing system was especially complex, and every few minutes I needed to ask for clarification. She was clearly becoming annoyed, but the job required some training. At the end of the day I said good-bye and added, "See you tomorrow," to which she replied, "You're coming back? I didn't think you liked us." I shrugged and left. The next day the quarterly report had come due. I stood at the main photocopy machine from 9:15 A.M. until lunch, and for another two hours and fifteen minutes afterwards. Every half hour I would carry a box of collated report copies back upstairs. When the project was finally completed, I sat down at the desk, sighed, and just closed my eyes in relief. I needed five minutes to re-group. She came rushing out of her office and said, loud enough for the other secretaries to hear, "Excuse me, but when you have down-time, I'd appreciate if you tell me so I can give you something else to do." I turned to her and said firmly, "Excuse me, but I've been on my feet for the whole day. I know I'm not wearing heels but I'm still entitled to sit for five minutes." She walked back into the office and closed the door.

At that moment, I called my counselor and asked for a different assignment. She said to stay calm and try to stick it out a bit longer. On Friday, at 4:53 P.M. I handed her my timesheet. She told me she wouldn't sign because I still "owed her" ten minutes. I went back to my desk, put on my jacket, zipped my knapsack, and folded my hands on the desk. When she did sign, she said, "I assume you're not coming back Monday." Before I could answer, she told me *she* wouldn't be in until Tuesday. Given this condition, I offered to come back just for that day, as my absence would put the other staff in a bind. I had a pleasant and productive day then, and made sure I shook hands with everyone when I left at 5:00.

Same Company Different Division

Sometimes you may be sent to different divisions within the same company. These experiences can be like night and day, depending upon the people you work with. Always treat re-assignment like an entirely new job, even if you know your way around the firm. The hospital with the terrific people I mentioned earlier also had a problem assignment. I was sent to the finance department, where the supervisor set me up at a work station and typed "123." Before I could react, a spreadsheet appeared on the screen. I felt very uncomfortable because I am still to this day a functional illiterate on spreadsheet programs. I can enter data into a prefabricated format, but that's about it.

The supervisor gave me hundreds of receipts to enter into the system. I didn't mind doing this sort of work, but I was expecting to be word processing on a MacIntosh® program. I called my counselor and told him the situation. His response was, "That's okay. You'll be a pro by the end of the week. Call me when the assignment's done." At noon, I reached for my jacket and told the boss I'd be back in an hour. She asked if I could just give her a hand with something before I left that "would only take a minute." What she needed was two additional columns added to the spreadsheet to give a percent differential and an annual forecast.

I was puzzled. I was just getting by with entering figures, but I knew nothing about advanced features. I apologized and told her I couldn't do any spreadsheet programming. "I told them to send me someone good," she snapped. I tilted my head forward and said, "They did, but I'm not a programmer." She asked what the difference is and I said $45 an hour. I politely reminded her the THC sent someone who can enter data as per the requisition. I suggested she call the MIS department and ask them for a programmer to set up the new template. When I returned from lunch, the spreadsheet had been amended and I was able to continue working. Politeness and resourcefulness won out.

Recapitulation

Is it correct to think of Temping as "US versus THEM?" I would have to discourage that kind of attitude. Temping is a business, not a contest. Anyone who Temps is a professional contingency worker responsible first and foremost to him or herself. This includes maintaining an honest and congenial relationship with your employer, whether it be a THC, consulting firm, leasing company, or the client itself.

Problems do arise, and Temps have to realize that they are at a disadvantage because they usually cannot deal directly with human resources departments. They also have real issues on their minds such as insurance and tax concerns, as well as the uncertainty of steady work. They meet all types of people and are expected to blend right in from the moment they appear on the job site. Sometimes they are considered odd and are mistrusted. Other times they are welcomed and respected for their abilities.

The three keys, Adaptability, Congeniality, and Professionalism, must be adhered to throughout your Temping career. Whenever possible, have your counselor, if appropriate, intervene in times of distress. If you are a freelancer, use discretion but never burn bridges behind you.

Temping provides a good income, a wealth of experiences, and an excellent opportunity to enhance and expand your skills, while allowing you to explore new career possibilities. Take advantage of what's out there, and at the same time keep your eyes and ears open to protect yourself and to "grow with the flow."

CHAPTER TWENTY-FOUR

Temping As The Wave Of The Future

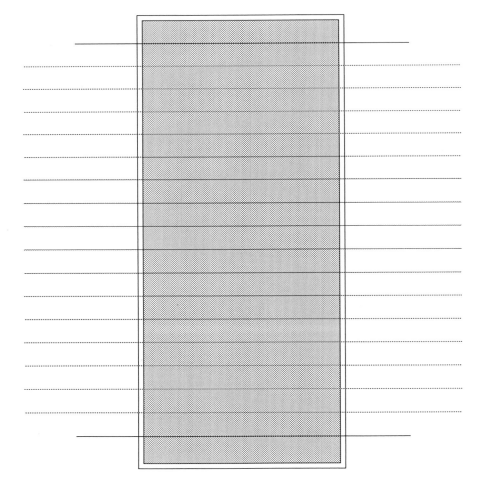

Today's client companies and THCs have needs and expectations that are fairly straightforward. Clients require instant, or "just-in-time," employees capable of everything—from washing windows, answering phones, making soufflés, programming computers, and dressing wounds—to the most traditional Temp act of all, typing memos. And to survive in a highly competitive market, THCs must perform a balancing act of baffling proportions. They interview thousands of candidates, select the most promising for their pools, and cross their fingers and bite the bullet in the hope that their judgment calls are to the advantage of their clients, and subsequently, to theirs and their Temps.

New Expectations

Gone forever are the days when oversized Ford autos and "Temp Mobiles" would chauffeur tall, slender, bouffanted, midi-skirted single young women off to the job site, with heavy, but nonetheless portable typewriters in hand. Likewise, THCs will never again set up on-site registration vans to lure suburban homemakers out of the kitchen and into the typing pool. No woman, or for that matter, no man, today would dare boast she or he is a "Kelly Girl," and no one in the post-War America of the 1940s and 1950s, Hip '60s, and Soft and Cool '70s, Temp and THC alike, imagined the government attention given to, and the economic ramifications of, the temporary employment industry.[2]

The work place has been revolutionized by the mechanical adding machine, the typewriter, (and electric versions thereof), the mainframe computer and subsequent birth of MIS, the dedicated word processor, and finally, the personal computer. Indeed, the office support Temp of the Future must be computer literate. Barbara Garson's engaging and most informative book *The Electronic Sweatshop* deals specifically with this decisive phenomenon.

Today's Temps need to take some responsibility for the way they are perceived. Everyone going out for Temp assignments needs to assume an appearance that does not distinguish. I have tried to stress that creative and "nontraditional" persons still have an obligation to show up dressed fittingly for whatever work environment to which they have been assigned. Whenever a Temp agrees to accept an assignment, that commitment must be honored to the best of his or her abilities. "Flexibility" does not mean license to ignore responsibility.

What do Temps want? The answer is simple. Temps want steady work, decent wages, and work environments where they are respected as professional contingency workers and as human beings. This is not much to ask for, and the gears have been in place for a long time. But the Temp of the future, living in a global economy, will require at least some of the benefits and safety nets taken for granted by our European counterparts. The greater the security net, the greater attention Temps can pay to their assignments. In return, they will be expected to be more exclusive in their relationships with THCs, and take every opportunity to learn new skills.

Foreign Temps

European Temps often have that special sense of exclusivity and prodigious loyalty. This can be attributed to the freshness of the industry outside the United States. In short, with fewer alternatives European Temps can often select those one or two THCs that best fit their needs and stay with them for most of their careers. Another reason is that many European nations provide universal safety nets. Affordable health insurance, generous unemployment benefits, pregnancy benefits, and educational grants are routine. The downside is that while Ireland, the United Kingdom, the Netherlands, Luxembourg, and Denmark permit their THCs to operate much like those in the United States, strict regulation is enforced in Belgium, France, and Germany.

Further, Temping as we understand it is currently **banned** in Greece, Italy, and Spain.[3] Regulation à la Common Market member nations means clients have to justify their requisitions. Only illness, maternity leave, special projects, and exceptional increases in workloads are valid reasons. And there's no overtime allowed. The good news is that in Belgium you get one month's paid vacation, and in France it's five weeks.

Coming back to our needs, perhaps in the near future we will see a convincing effort on the part of client companies to stop penalizing their long-term and in-house Temps for company half-days. I do not advocate paying Temps for legal holidays when the company is closed, but if a 3:00 P.M. shut-down has been enacted on the Friday before a holiday, I believe it's unjust to dock a Temp who has also shown up that day expecting a full day's work.

Temps of the future will come to expect periodic raises and bonus, vacation pay, and of course, some relief with health insurance premiums. To pay for the latter, perhaps a small surcharge will need to be added to client fees so the cost burden can be spread out. True, some THC's have responded early to these needs, but there is no universal canon. Government legislation may take into account some sort of burden sharing in the European tradition.

Consider this strategy.

> Josh is an expert word processing secretary who
> normally earns $17 an hour from his THC. The THC
> charges the client $25 an hour for his services, and
> uses the difference ($8) for operating expenses and
> profit. With a mandatory health insurance surcharge
> built in to all Temp transactions—which can come
> about either through legislation or convention a few
> years down the road—the client will now pay $25.50
> an hour for Josh's services, while the THC "donates"
> 25¢ on the hour out of the $8 "take", and in the end
> pays Josh $16.75 instead of $17, as he is required to
> meet a 25¢ deduction as well.
> A total of $1 has now been slated for Josh's health
> insurance account, with a breakdown contribution ratio
> of 2:1:1 on the parts of client, THC, and employee,
> respectively. This $1 is deposited in a government pre-
> tax, or better yet non-taxable, fund, so after one month
> of steady work at 35 hours per week, Josh's account
> has a principal of $140, derived from $1 an hour x 35
> hours x 4 weeks. Spread over the eleven months of
> actual days Josh works, the account will grow to $1540,
> of which Josh has contributed $385. If health care
> reform contains a non-taxable, high-yield interest
> account proviso, Josh will have even more money
> invested. He can then use that money to buy insurance
> for himself, making up any difference in premium
> from his own pocket.

However, in actuality we must wait and see what the government produces; hopefully, something like the above model is not just a pipedream. Nonetheless, THCs are nervous about health care reform, because as employers, they may have to put in an additional 7.9% of all payroll expenditures in premium contributions.[4] In addition, they justifiably are concerned about having to offer health insurance because premiums are usually paid monthly and there is no guarantee that a particular Temp will be on the company's payroll long enough during a given month to make this feasible. But if the system becomes universal, there can only be a greater commitment between counselor and Temp.

Perhaps a "Temp Union" will emerge in the next few years to serve as a lobbying group. We surely need it. Perhaps additional legislation will be paced. Finally, I foresee the end of "Temp Agreements" for in-house Temps wherever potential legal conflict is apparent. No one, Temp or otherwise, should be coerced or compelled to violate his or her rights just to enrich the coffers of an employer whose ethical agenda turns its back on State and Federal labor law.

These issues continue to be addressed by the national THCs and by NATSS. But two things are clear: (1) the temporary employment indus-try is rapidly growing; and (2) the onus is on us Temps to study the possibilities, discipline ourselves to acquire as many skills as possible, view ourselves as professional people, prove our abilities, take care of our bodies and minds, and never, ever think of ourselves or give anyone else reason to think of us as "just a Temp."

Notes

1. New Yorkers and other East Coasters find it anathema to use anything but the colloquialism "Temp agency;" however, the rest of us should not shun the more accurate terms "temporary employment service" and "temporary help company." "Agency," incidentally, is also the preferred journalistic term.

2. Janice Castro, "Disposable Workers," in Lance Morrow, "The Temping of America," *Time* (March 29, 1993): 43.

3. Beth Belton, "Industrial jobs go to service staff," *USA Today,* 13 September 1993, sec. B, p. 1.

4. Ida L. Walters, "Temping Fate," *Reason* (April 1994): 50.

5. Reported in John T. Ward, "Part-time, temporary jobs at unrelenting high levels," *Asbury Park Press,* 13 September 1993, sec. D, p. 4.

6. Walters, "Temping Fate," p. 50.

7. Ibid., p. 51.

8. Ibid.

9. As of November 23, 1993, businesses, contractors, and military personnel affected by base closings can contact a government clearinghouse for information regarding services available to them, including retraining programs. Called the "Economic Conversion Information Exchange," the voice-activated service is sponsored by the U.S. Department of Commerce. Tapes refer callers to information available by fax or on electronic systems such as computer bulletin boards and Internet.™ The toll-free number is 1–800–345–1222.

10. For an excellent overview of the innovative opportunities for actors in Temp pools see Ben Alexander, "Spotlight on Temporary Employment Services," *Back Stage,* 21 September 1990, p. 27ff; idem., "Offstage Opportunities for Performers," *Back Stage,* 18 September 1992, p. 2ff; idem., "Giving in to Temp-tation," *Back Stage,* 17 September 1993, p. 1ff; Holly Obernauer, "Temp Work & Performing Artists," *N.Y. Casting Magazine* (November 9, 1993): 4; and *Fraiser* co-star David Hyde Pierce's anecdotes about his stint as a legal Temp in *Legal Assistant Today* (March/April 1994): 29–30.

11. The results were published as "Profile of the Temporary Workforce," *Contemporary Times* (Spring 1994). Cf. with "Profile of a Typical Temporary Employee," *Contemporary Times* (Winter 1989). Contact NATSS for reprints.

12. As reported in the *Wall Street Journal,* 7 July 1993, sec. A, p. 1(E).
13. Martha T. Moore, "Philip Morris burns 14,000 jobs," *USA Today,* 26 November 1993, sec. B, p. 3.
14. *Wall Street Journal,* 8 December 1993, sec. A, p. 2(E) and *New York Times,* 8 December 1993, sec. D, p. 1.
15. John Holusha, "A Profitable Xerox Plans to Cut Staff by 10,000," *New York Times,* 9 December 1993, sec. D, p. 1(L), et al.
16. *Wall Street Journal,* 14 October 1993, sec. A, p. 3(E), and Ibid., 9 September 1994, sec. A, p. 3(E).
17. *Wall Street Journal,* 20 October 1993, sec. A, p. 3(E).
18. *Wall Street Journal,* sec. A, p. 1(E).
19. *Wall Street Journal,* 5 January 1994, sec. B, p. 6(E).
20. *Wall Street Journal,* 10 January 1994, sec. A, p. 2(E).
21. John J. Keller, "GTE to Trim 13% of Workers, Post Big Charge," *Wall Street Journal,* 14 January 1994, sec. A, p. 3(E).
22. Peter Gumbel, "Western Europe Finds That It's Pricing Itself Out of the Job Market," *Wall Street Journal,* 9 December 1993, sec. A, p. 1(E).
23. "Scott Paper Sets Plan to Cut 25% of Work Force," *Wall Street Journal,* 27 January 1994, sec. A, p. 1(E).
24. David R. Francis, "Corporations Begin 'Just in Time' Hiring," *Christian Science Monitor,* 6 May 1994, p. 11.
25. For an excellent overview of the impact of mismanaged conglomerates on the lives of American Workers, the layman is referred to Donald L. Bartlett and James B. Steele, *America: What Went Wrong?* (Kansas City: Andrews and McNeal, 1992).
26. Barbara Garson, "Permanent Temps," *The Nation* (June 1, 1992): 736.
27. See, for example, Anita Hussey, "Rent-A-Veep," *Executive Female* (May–June 1990): 14ff; Deidre Fanning, "The Temporary Answer to the Recession," *New York Times,* 16 December 1990, sec. 3, p. 25(L); and Laura Mansnerus, "Lawyer Layoffs: Boon to Temporary Jobs," *New York Times,* 3 May 1991, sec. B, p. 11(L).
28. Christina Duff, "In a Portland Hot Tub, Young Grads' Anxiety Bubbles to the Surface," *Wall Street Journal,* 7 July 1993, sec. A, p. 1(E).
29. Tony Horwitz, "Not Home Alone: Jobless Male Managers Proliferate in Suburbs, Causing Subtle Malaise," *Wall Street Journal,* 20 September 1993, sec. A, p. 1(E).
30. See, for example, Julie Amparano Lopez, "Many Early Retirees Find the Good Deals Not So Good After All," *Wall Street Journal,* 25 October 1993, sec. A, p. 1(E).
31. Lance Morrow, "The Temping of America," op. cit.
32. Jaclyn Fierman, "The Contingency Work Force," *Fortune* (January 24, 1994): 30–36.

33. Ann Crittenden, "Temporary Solutions," *Working Woman* (February 1994): 32ff.
34. Laura McClure, "Working the Risk Shift," *The Progressive* (February 1994): 23ff.
35. The misinterpretation of the Manpower, Inc. payroll numbers was identified by Ida L. Walters in her article "Temping Fate," op. cit.

Part Two

1. "How Much Should I Charge?," (Cincinnati: Writer's Digest Books, 1993), p. 46–48. With the kind permission of the publisher.
2. Compiled by Shari Caudron, "Focus: Benefits," in Allan Halcrow, "The HR Budget Squeeze," *Personnel Journal* (June 1992): 126.
3. See in this regard Terry E. Schraeder and Mark D. Dore, "A Pay Formula for the '90s," *Personnel Journal* (October 1990): 46–47.
4. Ibid.
5. Entitled the "Reemployment Act," House Bill 4040, sponsored by Dan Roustenkowski (D–IL) and William D. Ford (D–MI) was submitted "to establish a comprehensive system of reemployment services, training, and income support for permanently laid off workers, to facilitate the establishment of one-stop career centers to serve as a common point of access to employment, education, and training information and services, and to develop an effective national labor market information system." It cleared the House Human Resources Subcommittee on July 22, 1994, and at the time of writing is under review by the Trade Subcommittee. A Senate version (S–1951) was presented by Senators Daniel Patrick Moynihan (D–NY), George Mitchell (D–ME), et al.
6. NB: If you're laid off from a full-time position and qualify for unemployment insurance, investigate your state's laws before you register with a THC, because this might disqualify you altogether.
7. Employers should note the following articles: Bill Montague, "IRS cracks down on use of contractors," *USA Today,* 21 March 1991, sec. B, p. 8; Richard Weatherington, "IRS cracks down on employee misclassification," *Public Relations Journal* (February 1992): 30–32; and Ani Hadjian, "Hiring Temps Full-Time May Get the IRS on Your Tail," *Fortune* (24 January 1994): 34.
8. See, for example, Vanessa Gallman and Frank McCoy, "How to Choose the Best Health Plan for You," *Black Enterprise* (November 1990): 71ff.
9. An interesting article that spotlights the disparate insurance needs and pursuits of two people in Andrée Brooks, "Adrift in the Market for Health Insurance," *New York Times,* 11 September 1993, p. 35(L).
10. I should like to thank Mr. John A. Radovich of Time Insurance Company for detailing the various policies offered by his firm.

11. Quoted from the Albert H. Wohlers & Co. brochure offered to NATSS-affiliated THCs and their employees. I should also like to thank Kathleen Trautmann and Jesse Bozman of Albert H. Wohlers & Co. for discussing the policies with me by telephone.

Part Three

1. The following has been summarized succinctly in Susan Avery, "Shorthanded? Hire a Temp," *Purchasing* (March 22, 1990): 70ff.

2. NATSS Fact Sheet—June 24, 1993. Quoted with the kind permission of Bruce Steinberg, NATSS Media Relations Manager.

3. For the full listing, see Kate Evans-Correia, "Temp work industry reflects economic times," *Purchasing* (August 13, 1992): 84–85.

4. (White Hall, VA: Betterway Publications, Inc., 1985), p. 26.

5. Bob Herbert, "When job agency waives 'Help Not Wanted' Sign, *Daily News*, 1 June 1989, p. 4, and idem., "'All-American' Tint is our town's bias," *Daily News*, 15 August 1989, p. 4.

6. Christy Marshall, "Some Job Agencies 'Code' by Race, Sex, Age, Looks," *New York Newsday*, 26 June 1989, sec. III, p. 10–11.

7. See Wayne E. Barrow and Edward Z. Hane, "A Practical Guide to the Americans with Disabilities Act," *Personal Journal* (June, 1992): 53–60; Laura M. Litvan, "The Disabilities Law: Avoid the Pitfalls," *Nation's Business* (January 1994): 25–27; and Carl Quintanilla, "Disabilities Act Helps—But Not Much," *Wall Street Journal*, 19 July 1993, sec. B, p. 1(E).

8. Data compiled by Stephen Conley and published in *USA Today*, 22 July 1993, sec. A, p. 1.

9. Wade Lambert, "Obese Workers Win On-the-Job Protection Against Bias" (1B).

10. Derived from William Atkinson's insightful article, "Temporary Employees: The Demand Exceeds the Supply," *The Office* (May 1990): 59–60.

11. On client-agency interaction, see Bernard Howroyd, "Hidden Agendas for Temporary Services," *HR Magazine* (September 1990): 51ff.

Notes

Part Four

1. Karen Mendenhall, in her book *Making the Most of the Temporary Employment Market* (Cincinnati: Betterway Books, 1993), relates several responses to this question, such as her quotation of a Temp who, upon notice of termination owing to budget concerns, said, "Oh, I'll sit at home in my ratty bathrobe and fuzzy slippers and eat bonbons" (p. 115).

Part Five

1. Published in *The Washington Post*, 30 April 1993, sec. A, p. 25.
2. As this book has not discussed the history of the industry, the reader is referred the excellent monograph of Martha I. Finney and Deborah A. Dasch, *A Heritage of Service* (Alexandria, VA: National Association of Temporary Services, 1991).
3. As reported by Max Messmer in "Temporary Employees Are Permanent Part of New Europe," *Personnel Journal* (January 1994): 100–101.
4. "Temps to cost more?" *Asbury Park Press*, 24 December 1993, sec. B, p. 6.

For Further Reading

Temporary Employment and Consulting

Broudy, Eve. *Professional Temping, A Guide to Bridging Career Gaps.* Collier Books, 1989.

Fanning, John with Sullivan, G. *Work When You Want To: The Complete Guide for the Temporary Worker.* New York: Macmillan; R., Pocket Books, 1985.

Idem., and Maniscalco, R. *Workstyles to Fit Your Lifestyle: Everyone's Guide to Temporary Employment.* Englewood Cliffs, NJ: Prentice Hall, 1993.

Finney, Martha I. and Dasch, D.A. *A Heritage of Service.* Alexandria, VA: National Association of Temporary Services, 1991.

Holtz, Herman. *The Complete Work-At-Home Companion.* Rocklin, CA: Prima Publishing and Communications, 1990.

Justice, Peggy O'Connell. *The Temp Track: Make One of the Hottest Job Trends for the 90's Work for You.* Princeton, NJ: Peterson's, 1994.

Lewis, William M. and Molloy, N.H. *How to Choose and Use Temporary Services.* New York: American Management Association (Amacom), 1991.

Idem., and Schuman, N. *The Temp Worker's Handbook: How to Make Temporary Employment Work for You.* New York: Amacom, 1988.

Mendenhall, Karen. *Making the Most of the Temporary Employment Market.* Cincinnati: Betterway Books, 1993.

Smith, Deborahann. *Temp: How to Survive and Thrive in the World of Temporary Employment.* Boston: Shambhala, 1994.

Smith, Demaris C. *Temporary Employment: The Flexible Alternative.* White Hall, VA: Betterway Publications, 1985.

Other Books of Interest

Bloch, Deborah. *How to Get a Good Job and Keep It.* Lincolnwood: VGM Career Horizons, 1993.

Bolles, Richard Nelson. *What Color Is Your Parachute?* Berkeley: Ten Speed Press, 1993.

Bramson, Robert. *Coping with Difficult Bosses.* New York: Birch Lane Press, 1992.

Brown, Duane. *How to Find a New Career Upon Retirement.* Lincolnwood: VGM Career Horizons, 1995.

Cetron, Marvin and Davies, O. *The Great Job Shake-Out.* New York: Simon and Schuster, 1988.

Clemens, Lynda and Dolph, A. *How to Hit the Ground Running in Your New Job.* Lincolnwood: VGM Career Horizons, 1995.

Figler, Howard. *The Complete Job-Search Handbook.* New York: Henry Holt and Co., 1988.

Foster, Stanley. *Toxic Executives.* New York: Harper Business, 1993.

Freedman, Howard S. *How to Get a Headhunter to Call.* New York: John Wiley & Sons, 1989.

Garson, Barbara. *The Electronic Sweatshop.* New York: Simon and Schuster, 1988.

Gorkin, Jess. *Finding the Right Job at Midlife.* New York: Simon and Schuster, 1985.

Helfand, David. *Career Change: Everything You Need to Know to Meet New Challenges and Take Control of Your Career.* Lincolnwood: VGM Career Horizons, 1995.

Langhorne, Karyn E. and Martin, E. *Cover Letters They Don't Forget.* Lincolnwood: VGM Career Horizons, 1994.

Patterson, Martha Priddy. *The Working Woman's Guide to Financial Planning: Saving and Investing Now for a Secure Future.* Englewood Cliffs: Prentice Hall, 1993.

Petras, Katherine and Petras, R. *The Over-40 Job Guide.* New York: Poseidon Press, 1993.

Provenzano, Steven. *Slam Dunk Resumes That Score Every Time.* Lincolnwood: VGM Career Horizons, 1994.

Wright, John W. *The American Almanac of Jobs and Salaries.* New York: Avon Books, 1993.